The Natural History of South Africa;
Mammals

THE NATURAL HISTORY
OF SOUTH AFRICA

The Vervet Monkey or Blaauw-aapje which inhabits the forests
of South Africa.

THE NATURAL HISTORY OF SOUTH AFRICA

INCLUDING THE VERVET MONKEYS, BABOONS, GALAGOS, FRUIT
BATS, INSECTIVOROUS BATS, LIONS, LEOPARDS, SERVAL
CATS, BLACK FOOTED CATS, AFRICAN WILD CATS
CARACALS, AND HUNTING LEOPARDS

BY

F. W. FITZSIMONS, F.Z.S., F.R.M.S., &c.

DIRECTOR, PORT ELIZABETH MUSEUM

MAMMALS

IN FOUR VOLUMES

VOL. I

LONGMANS, GREEN AND CO.

39 PATERNOSTER ROW, LONDON, E.C. 4

FOURTH AVENUE AND 30TH STREET, NEW YORK

BOMBAY, CALCUTTA, AND MADRAS

1919

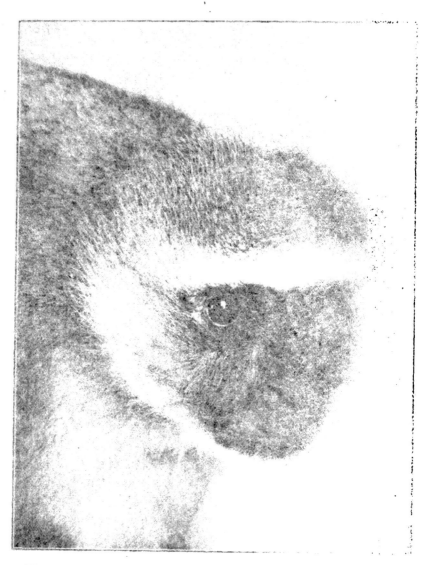

The Vervet Monkey or Blaauw-aapje wh.... ....
of South Africa.

THE NATURAL HISTORY
OF SOUTH AFRICA

INCLUDING THE VERVET MONKEYS, BABOONS, GALAGOS, FRUIT
BATS, INSECTIVOROUS BATS, LIONS, LEOPARDS, SERVAL
CATS, BLACK-FOOTED CATS, AFRICAN WILD CATS
CARACALS, AND HUNTING LEOPARDS

BY

F. W. FITZSIMONS, F.Z.S., F.R.M.S., &c.
DIRECTOR, PORT ELIZABETH MUSEUM

MAMMALS

IN FOUR VOLUMES

VOL. I

LONGMANS, GREEN AND CO.
39 PATERNOSTER ROW, LONDON, E.C. 4
FOURTH AVENUE AND 30TH STREET, NEW YORK
BOMBAY, CALCUTTA, AND MADRAS

1919

TO

MY WIFE

WHO HAS SHARED MY LABOURS I DEDICATE

THESE BOOKS

PREFACE

THE series of volumes of which this is the first are intended to supply information about the ways and habits of the creatures of veld, forest, mountain, and stream, so that school teachers, senior pupils, and the general public may have a ready means of learning to distinguish friend from foe in the lower animal kingdom.

Wherever civilised man penetrates he destroys the native animals and birds indiscriminately. His children are encouraged to sally forth with catapult, air gun, and shot gun and wantonly destroy the lives of innocent and often eminently useful creatures. He even encourages them to make collections of the eggs of wild birds, thereby diminishing the numbers of insectivorous birds which are of immense economic value to the country.

When I think of my youthful days, I burn with shame and remorse, for, in the light of knowledge subsequently gained, I am conscious of having taken the lives of numbers of animals and birds of great economic value, and the lives of many others, although of little or no value economically, yet innocent of harm as far as man is concerned.

If the knowledge which I now possess of the ways and habits of the lower animals had been acquired in early boyhood, I should have, in consequence, exercised greater discrimination in the destruction of animal life.

It cannot be too often reiterated that considerable numbers of the animals, birds, and reptiles of our country are of great economic value, and to kill them is a crime against our neighbours, and those of our kind who come after us.

In the more populous centres of civilisation, where the native animals have been allowed to be destroyed indiscriminately and ignorantly, the annual financial losses both direct and indirect are great.

It is not only the farmer and gardener who suffer financially. Every section of the community or of the State suffers, either directly or indirectly. For instance, if the species of birds and animals which prey upon the native rats and mice of this country were exterminated, these rodents would increase so rapidly that they would, in a very short space of time, swarm over the land and destroy the crops and even the native vegetation. This would impoverish the farmers and make agriculture unprofitable; and all branches of industry would, in consequence, suffer.

Even the Government revenue would considerably diminish by reason of the shrinkage of the import and export trade, and the general lessened

PREFACE

spending power of the citizens of the State. Artificial means, costing an immense annual expenditure of money, are taken in most countries with the object of endeavouring to combat the hosts of insect and other pests which keep back progress, development, and expansion. The necessity for such expenditure, or at least a considerable proportion of it, has arisen through allowing the insectivorous birds and useful animals to be wantonly destroyed or driven away. In the more populous centres of civilisation it is now too late to preach this gospel of the conservation of animals, birds, and reptiles useful to man; but not so in South Africa, and many other countries where civilised man has not yet become fully established.

The object aimed at in the series of books I am now engaged upon during my leisure hours is to furnish reliable information about the ways and habits of the animals with which we so frequently come in contact, and which we often so foolishly maim and kill.

From an early age I have been accumulating the facts which are set forth in this book, and which will be detailed in subsequent volumes.

This set of books was ready for publication in 1914, but owing to the war their publication was deferred. The opportunity has been taken to revise them and introduce fresh facts and illustrations.

To Mr. W. L. Sclater is due the honour of first

NATURAL HISTORY OF SOUTH AFRICA

gathering together in book form the records of the animals of South Africa, and to him I am indebted for many facts and descriptions in this volume. To the advanced student of Natural History, his two volumes entitled *The Fauna of South Africa* are a valuable aid. I am also indebted to Dr. Oldfield Thomas, F.R.S., and Mr. M. A. C. Hinton of the British Museum (Natural History), for their kindness in revising the Systematic Index.

THE AUTHOR.

PORT ELIZABETH, 1919.

SYSTEMATIC INDEX
OF THE ANIMALS IN VOLUME I

Order : PRIMATES
Sub-order : Anthropoidea
Family : CERCOPITHECIDÆ
Genus : *Cercopithecus*

Sub-order : Lemuroidea
Family : LEMURIDÆ
Sub-family : Galaginæ
Genus : *Galago*

2. *Pipistrellus nanus australis.* (Sub-species of No. 1.)
3. *Pipistrellus kuhlii fuscatus,* Thos.
4. *Pipistrellus subtilis,* Sund.
5. *Pipistrellus rusticus,* Tomes.

Genus : *Glauconycteris*
(The Butterfly Bats)

1. *Glauconycteris variegatus,* Tomes. (*Chalinolobus variegatus* of Sclater).
2. *Glauconycteris papilio,* Thos.

Genus : *Scotophilus*
(Dobson's Bats)

1. *Scotophilus nigrita,* Schreb.
2. *Scotophilus nigrita dinganii,* Smith, Pet. (Sub-species of No. 1.)
3. *Scotophilus nigrita herero,* Thos. (Sub-species of No. 1.)
4. *Scotophilus viridis damarensis,* Thos.

Genus : *Scoteinus*

1. *Scoteinus schlieffeni australis,* Thos. and Wrought.

Genus : *Myotis*
(The Mouse-eared Bats)

1. *Myotis tricolor,* Smuts.

Genus : *Kerivoula*

1. *Kerivoula ærosa,* Tomes. The Bronze Bat.
2. *Kerivoula lanosa,* Smith. The Woolly Bat.
3. *Kerivoula brunnea,* Chubb.

Genus : *Miniopterus*
(The Long-winged Bats)

1. *Miniopterus schreibersi,* Kuhl.
2. *Miniopterus dasythrix,* Temm.

SYSTEMATIC INDEX

ILLUSTRATIONS

xvii

NATURAL HISTORY OF SOUTH AFRICA

ILLUSTRATIONS

Vervet Monkey lying concealed.

(*a*) When attempts are made to shoot Vervet Monkeys aloft
amongst the branches of a great forest tree, they lie flat
along the branches, as seen in this picture, and are invisible
to the man with the gun below.

Vervet Monkey lying concealed.

(*b*) When lying on my back under a great forest tree I would often
observe Vervet Monkeys peering over a branch with timid
frightened black faces. On the slightest movement on my
part the faces would instantly vanish.

THE NATURAL HISTORY OF SOUTH AFRICA

THE VERVET MONKEY OR BLUE APE

(*Cercopithecus pygerythrus*)
Syn.: *C. lalandii*

Also known as the Inkau of Amaxosa and Zulus (*Stanford and Kirby*); Ingobiyana of Swazis (*Kirby*); Inkalat-shana of Basutos (*Kirby*).

THERE are two distinct tribes of monkeys in South Africa—the Rock-climbing Baboons and the Arboreal Monkeys.

The home of the Vervet or Blue Ape is in the forest belts, chiefly on the eastern side of South Africa, from Swellendam in the Cape Province to the Transvaal, and along the wooded banks of the larger rivers. Troops of these apes are, however, often met with in patches of dense bush in various inland districts. At times Vervet Monkeys venture out upon the veld in search of food, a few hundreds of yards from their leafy home ; but on the slightest cause for alarm they scamper off and take cover in the trees, where it is useless to pursue them ; for, up amongst the branches of the great forest trees, they are at home, travelling over the tree-tops at great speed, making astonishing leaps at times with hands and feet spread out ready to grip the nearest branch. Although possessing long tails, the Vervets never use them for gripping tree branches—the tails are not prehensile, as is the case with their cousins, the American monkeys.

They are adepts at concealment, and when lying along the thick branches of tall forest trees, flattened down and immovable, they cannot be observed from below; nor is it, as a general rule, possible to shoot them when they peep over the side of a branch.

The Vervet Monkeys associate in troops of from a dozen to about a hundred individuals of both sexes and all ages. The adult males are at all times jealous of each other, and frequent battles are fought. The male, whose strength and fighting powers are superior to the others, assumes leadership, which he holds just so long as he is physically superior to the other males in the troop, who fight at intervals among themselves, until one eventually proves himself superior to the rest. Then he gives battle to the leader, and should he succeed in vanquishing him, he becomes supreme chief. If the old leader happens to have escaped with his life, he is doomed for the rest of his existence to live in solitude. "Might is Right" in the lower animal world.

THE VERVET MONKEY OR BLUE APE

This fierce fighting amongst male animals for the right to perpetuate the species is a safeguard against physical deterioration. It is indeed a bitter struggle for the survival of the fittest, but none can question the wisdom of it.

The males who from time to time are driven into exile, live lonely, celibate lives, becoming morose and exceedingly cunning and daring. They usually take to robbing the agriculturalist and fruit-grower of the hard-earned products of his labour. So intelligently are these raids planned, that it is the exception for the exasperated farmer to succeed in encompassing the death of the thief.

Unfortunately it is not only the solitary individuals who rob man of the fruits of his industry. The cultivated fields of farmers are invaded by whole troops of these monkeys, and lamentable havoc is wrought. Nothing in the way of vegetable produce or fruit comes amiss to them. They are wasteful in the extreme, and it is indeed no wonder the agriculturalist regards them as one of the most destructive forms of vermin. Many species of animals eat to satisfy their hunger, and are not in the least wasteful; others dine generously and carry off a portion and lay it aside for lean times ; but not so the monkey tribe.

Many scores of times I have seen the results of raids on orchards and crops by Vervet Monkeys. On one occasion a troop of a hundred or more of them visited a mealie field at dawn. The mealies on the cobs were in the soft, sweet, and milky stage of development. Three sentinels were on duty, for, owing to the nature of the surroundings, one could not command a sufficiently extensive view to prevent the possibility of enemies stealing up unseen. The moment we turned the corner of the neighbouring forest, loud warning cries rang out from the sentinels, and off scampered the troops of thieves, each with a cob or two in their hands. Arriving on the scene of the feast, we found hundreds of mealie cobs littered over the ground, and many scores more hanging torn and broken from the stems. Not a single cob had the mealies entirely eaten off it. Like pampered children sampling an assortment of sweets and cakes, these apes merely tore with their teeth some of the sheath; took a bite at the mealies, and, if not sweet enough for their liking, another was torn from the stem and sampled ; and so on until a sufficiently sweet and milky one was discovered. Then, with a grunt of satisfaction it would be partly devoured, and another sought. The ground was strewn with mealie cobs, and the stems in all directions had been broken down to get at the cobs, which are usually high up on the stem of the plant.

This particular troop of apes lived in a neighbouring kloof, the bottom and sides of which were densely clothed with thick tangled bush, mostly of the kind bristling with long sharp thorns. In this wild retreat the monkeys were safe from their human enemies, and they knew it perfectly well. From the

Vervet Monkeys (*Cercopithecus pygerythrus*). Male, female, and twins. When the female was captured, she had two babies about a month old, which clung tightly to her breast.

trees at the top of the kloof they were able to observe the approach of an enemy, afar off. They were altogether too wise to plan their raids always at the same time of day. Knowing the humanfolk were not nocturnal by habit, and that they were invariably safely in bed asleep by midnight, the monkeys would steal forth in the grey dawn of the morning and during moonlight nights, and lay waste the crops. Seldom were the fields visited twice in succession at the same hour. Watching their chance when the farm labourers were at a safe distance, the entire troop, at a given signal from the leader, would make a sudden dash from cover in broad daylight; and, stuffing their cheek pouches full of provender from the fields, and seizing a mealie cob or two in the hands, and another with the jaws, they would make off to their forest retreat.

However, they did not always have it all their own way. The farmer and his sons were busy scheming to get even with them. Poisoned food and traps had failed—a few inexperienced juveniles had fallen victims to the poison and traps, but these apes are worldly wise—yes, wiser than many of the humanfolk, for they profit by experience; and no matter how cleverly and temptingly the farmer laid the poisoned bait; or how cunningly he concealed the nature of his traps, the monkeys were too cunning and observant, and their senses of taste and smell were far too acute to allow of them being lured to their death in these ways. If some new means of trapping them

5

was discovered and put into practice, a few, possibly, of the troop would fall victims ; but one such experience was invariably sufficient, for the whole troop would be evermore specially on their guard against the new danger. The farmer, in this instance, was as ingenious in his devices to destroy the monkeys, as they were in planning out ways to steal his produce. Observing that the raids usually took place in the early hours of the morning, excepting on nights when the moon was shining brightly, the harassed farmer took a gang of labourers with picks and shovels to the scene of the robberies. He sent his sons off in advance with the dogs to the edge of the forest, at the top of the kloof in which the troop of monkeys lived in security, to make a demonstration in order to scare them down into the heart of the bush at the bottom of the kloof, where they could not command a view of the mealie fields. Then he set his men to work and excavated half a dozen pits. These he carefully covered with mealie stalks. During the remainder of the day a man was kept in the vicinity, busy hoeing. This was with the object of deceiving the monkeys, and preventing them from discovering the pits.

A couple of hours before dawn, a party consisting of the farmer, his three sons, two sturdy daughters, and half a dozen half-caste Hottentots, stole silently through the mealie field, slipped into the pits, arranged the stalks and waited. Shortly after dawn the advance guard of the troop of monkeys appeared.

This is an albino Vervet Monkey (*C. pygerythrus*). It was captured and exhibited alive for a considerable time in a cage in the Port Elizabeth Museum. Its face was blotched black and pink, and there were a few small patches of normal monkey colour on its body.

THE VERVET MONKEY OR BLUE APE

They came along chattering and frolicking, confident their sentinels would give the alarm in good time if danger threatened. Entering the mealie field they scattered, each monkey intent upon eating to reple- tion of the succulent young mealies. Presently the chattering and practical joking turned to screams of wild alarm, for, from those six pits the reports of a dozen guns rang out with a deafening roar, followed by a second volley, for every gun was double-bar- relled. Three of the guns were breech-loaders, and before the horrified apes could gain sanctuary, another shower of loopers raked them. The sight was sickening in the extreme. A dozen or more monkeys lay dead, and others were lying wounded and helpless, or endeavouring to drag themselves to some place of concealment, while the coloured men, yelling like fiends, chased and slew them.

One of the wounded was a mother monkey; she' had been struck in the lower part of her back by a slug, and her hindquarters were paralysed. She clasped a baby in her arms, and was begging piteously for life—for the life of her child. Casting both arms around it, she made the most frantic efforts to shield it with her body. Looking over her shoulder she glared at her enemies, the muscles of her face assum- ing a variety of forms, and her teeth glittered in the early morning light. Those who have seen the grimacing of a mother monkey defending her child, are never likely to forget the sight.

Presently the menacing mien subsided; she

ceased to chatter in a threatening way. Her face relaxed, softened, and she gazed at her enemies with a piteous expression in her eyes, meanwhile giving vent to a succession of low mutterings which sounded sad and plaintive. It was evident she was appealing to the higher emotions of her enemies.

Tears gathered in my eyes, and a lump seemed to rise in my throat, and I turned and walked away, unable to bear the sight, for I knew the most merciful thing to do was to put her out of her misery. We took the terror-stricken, wizen-faced babe from her dead body, and wended our way back to the homestead, feeling mean and guilty. There was no rejoicing over our victory at the breakfast table. Each of us still seemed to see the face of that dying mother monkey, and hear her plaintive voice begging for the life of her child.

It seems an outrage on the part of Nature on our higher feelings, in fact on all that is human in us, to be compelled at times to slay without mercy various forms of the lower animals, which, according to the findings of modern men of science, are examples of the stock from which we have sprung, being after all our humble relatives, who do but seek to carry out the mission for which they were evolved.

However, it is necessary at times to sternly suppress all sentiment, unless we desire to retire from the face of the earth, and give it over to sub-human forms of life.

So long as monkeys live far away from the habitations of man, they are fulfilling the mission in life for which they were created ; but men and monkeys cannot live in proximity, for the latter are not sufficiently evolved to understand the rights of property from our point of view. No doubt the monkey tribe regard us as interlopers who have dispossessed them of some of their most valuable hunting-grounds, inherited from remote ancestors.

The ordinary fare of the Vervet Monkey is a meagre one. It consists of wild fruits, berries, tender shoots, sweet bark, flowers, bulbs, roots, the seeds and gum of the mimosa tree, various species of insects, birds' eggs, and the nestlings. All these items of monkey menu have to be shared with a host of other creatures ; and in times of drought there is by no means sufficient for all.

Apart from the damage done to crops, the Vervet Monkeys do man considerable indirect harm, in eating the eggs and nestlings of insectivorous birds, which, it is almost needless to say, are of great economic value.

In regard to insects, the balance of harm and the reverse is about even, from an economic point of view. Monkeys devour great numbers of caterpillars, chrysalides, and vegetable-eating beetles ; but on the contrary they eat insects such as spiders, which are the allies of Man in his war against the insect hosts which carry disease germs, or attack his crops.

Early one morning in Natal, a large troop of monkeys raided an orchard at a farm where I was staying. The havoc wrought was most disheartening to the owner. The ground was strewn with fruit, knocked down by the jumping of the monkeys amongst the branches; hundreds of apples and other kinds of fruit, with pieces bitten out of them, also lay around. The human race as a whole has much to thank the pioneer farmer for. It is he to a great extent who makes it possible for others of his race to colonise the earth. Settling in a new country, he is beset, as a general rule, by savage hordes of uncivilised men; carnivorous animals, which seek to rob him of his stock; and hosts of other animals which hover around, ever ready to appropriate the produce of his fields, orchards, and vegetable gardens. Unfortunately he is not always alive to the economic value of many forms of life around him, and consequently destroys, and allows his children and employees to destroy, birds, mammals, and reptiles which are his most valuable allies.

The Addo Bush near Port Elizabeth is the home of a number of troops of Vervet Monkeys. In the winter time they may be seen in scores sunning themselves on the tree-tops. During the months of December and January I observed numbers of females with babies clinging to them. There are no streams or springs of water in this extensive bushland, and, during times of drought, the apes are so hard pressed for water that they venture right up to the homesteads of farmers in search of

Three Vervet Monkeys squabbling over a mealie.

it. At these times food is so scarce that numbers perish, while the remainder become lank and lean.

On stock farms the Vervet Monkeys render excellent service in clearing the herbage of a variety of insect pests, including locusts. The bush-dwelling antelopes and Vervet Monkeys often fraternise. They descend from the trees and relieve the bucks of vermin. This is a sight which few have seen, for both antelopes and apes have the keenest of sight and hearing, while the former have the added gift of acute scent.

Lying motionless under a dense shrub watching a glade, and waiting to observe whatever form of life might venture from the surrounding thicket, I have seen Duikers and Bushbucks venture forth and fraternise with one another. Anon the monkeys dropped down from the trees and began hunting through the fur of the bucks for vermin, which they ate ; the antelopes meanwhile standing or lying calmly and at their ease. The observation of the denizens of mountain, forest, veld, and stream, without oneself being noticed, requires an unlimited stock of patience.

In Natal the Vervet Monkey used to be a great pest to the natives, as well as European farmers, and in many places it is still a nuisance. I have seen entire fields of mealies, kafir corn, pumpkins, sweet potatoes, orchards, and kitchen gardens destroyed by them, the owners being more or less powerless against these cunning, secretive, highly intelligent, and agile folk.

On one occasion a troop of Vervets were almost completely wiped out of existence. It was at Table Mountain, near Pietermaritzburg, in Natal. The Kafirs had been driven to desperation by a large troop of monkeys which inhabited a neighbouring wooded kloof. The bush was dense and thorny, and the ground broken and rocky, making it practically impossible for a man to penetrate it. Here the monkeys had a secure retreat, from which they usually issued at dawn, or on moonlight nights, to raid the crops of the natives. The Kafirs in the vicinity of the kloof had ceased to do any planting, owing to the depredations of the monkeys. Having acquired a liking for succulent milky mealies, the monkey troop took to raiding some fields at a distance, to get to which they were obliged to traverse some open grassy land, studded here and there with thorn trees. The monkeys had begun to look upon the Kafirs with contempt, more or less, for they had long since realised how impotent they were with their assegais and knob kerries. However, in the Kafir they had a crafty foe. In the dead of night about 300 Kafirs, armed with kerries, assegais, and sticks, assembled with their dogs. The mouths of the animals were tied with soft, raw-hide thongs, to prevent them barking. The army was divided into two portions, which took cover in dense thickets on each side of the wooded kloof. When the

A mother Vervet Monkey and her baby. When small the faces of the babies are pink. There is usually one at a birth. On rare occasions two.

first faint reflection from the sun tinged the sky on the horizon, the monkeys were astir, and with the greatest secrecy, and in absolute silence, they stole out of their forest home, intent upon breakfasting on mealies. The leader of the troop, who was a big fellow a third larger than any of the others, was well in advance, ready to give an alarm should he deem it necessary.

A Kafir securely hidden amongst some boulders on an adjacent elevation gave the agreed-upon signal —the hoot of an eagle-owl. Instantly the dogs were unmuzzled, and the two bodies of men spread out and met, forming a cordon across the mouth of the kloof ; while those towards the extremities of the line, advanced forward at a more rapid pace than those in the centre, forming a crescent-shaped line. The monkeys, finding themselves cut off from their forest home, chattered and screamed shrilly. Then a general rush was made away from that menacing line of Kafirs and dogs. No sooner had they started off than another body of men and boys started up from amidst the grass, and advanced on them. The troop of terror-stricken monkeys turned quickly about, broke and scattered, each individual intent upon saving himself. Some took refuge in the isolated mimosa trees, others raced blindly away, or frantically dashed at the line of black men and dogs between them and their sanctuary. A few eluded the kerries and assegais, and escaped into the kloof. Others were run down by the dogs, and desperate encounters occurred, which were terminated, in most instances, by the thrust of an assegai. Then the natives closed in on the monkeys cowering in the trees, and destroyed them. Out of a troop of about a hundred individuals, not more than a dozen escaped.

The chief of the native tribe, to celebrate the occasion, caused three oxen to be killed, and a feast was held, with the usual imbibing of great quantities of " Kafir beer," and subsequent quarrelling. For a couple of years afterwards the wearing apparel of those Kafirs consisted, chiefly, of the prepared skins of the slain monkeys, which were worn as aprons, known as Umutsha.

Vervet Monkeys are very numerous in the thick bush along the coast of Natal. From these retreats they issue forth and levy a heavy toll on the fruit gardens which are so abundant in the coastal districts.

In the forest belts along the coast on the eastern side of the Cape Province, the Vervets are also numerous. They may be seen almost daily within a few miles of Port Elizabeth. In riding round a corner on Schoenmaakers' Kop road, I dashed amongst a troop, which were at the time in the act of crossing the road, I noticed that several of them carried babies, which were held tight to the breast with one hand.

A troop of about half a hundred of these monkeys made frequent raids on a field of corn at Mount Pleasant, which is just beyond a township known as

THE VERVET MONKEY OR BLUE APE

Walmer. There was one leader to the troop, who was conspicuous by reason of his unusually large size, being at least a third bigger than any of the rest. The owner of the corn succeeded in shooting him, whereupon the rest of the troop disappeared from the neighbourhood, and have not been seen since.

Often when lying on my back, resting during the noonday heat in a forest in Natal, I saw inquisitive black faces peering down at me from the high branches of some tall tree. If I raised my hand or moved in any other way, every face instantly vanished amongst the foliage, or behind a branch. Often the monkeys lay flat along a branch and peered over the side, two eyes and a glimpse of a black brow only being visible from below. I frequently encountered troops of Vervets in the strips of bush bordering the banks of rivers. In fact in the inland districts in Natal I seldom saw them elsewhere than in the fringe of bush along watercourses ; or else in' the forests or wooded kloofs adjacent to rivers. When danger threatens, or when desiring to cross to the opposite bank of a stream, the Vervet Monkeys have no hesitation in plunging into the water and swimming across. I startled a large troop of these apes one day in the bush on the bank of the Umgeni River, in Natal. With loud cries of alarm they swung themselves up a tall tree, one of the topmost branches of which spread out over the stream. Running along to the end of this branch, the apes, one at a time, in rapid succession, sprang with hands and legs outspread and tail straight out behind, a distance of twenty feet or more into the top of a smaller tree on the opposite bank. It was a most interesting sight to see them leaping so gracefully, and with such apparent ease.

The chief enemies of Vervet Monkeys are leopards, caracals, servals, pythons, and the larger eagles, such as the Martial Eagle (*Eutolmœtus bellicosus*), Crowned Hawk-Eagle (*Spizœtus coronatus*), Verreaux's Eagle (*Aquila verreauxi*), African Hawk-Eagle (*Eutolmœtus spilogaster*).

The affection of the mother monkey for her baby is so great that it dominates her completely. When danger threatens she quite forgets herself in her anxiety for the safety of her helpless offspring. I was with a Dutch farmer friend in Natal one day, when we happened to surprise some monkeys in the orchard. They sprang in haste to the ground, and made off to the adjacent thorny thicket. The dogs gave chase, and a female with a rather heavy youngster in her arms, could not keep pace with the rest, and realising that it was impossible to reach the safety of the thicket in time, sprang up an isolated tree, and in a moment the dogs were howling at her from below. I tried to dissuade my friend from shooting at her, but he was so exasperated by the damage wrought by these monkeys from time to time, that he raised his gun and fired. Seeing him in the act of firing, the mother monkey swung round, placing her body between the gun and her

A baby Vervet Monkey, born in the Port Elizabeth Museum.
His face was wrinkled and drawn like that of an aged
Hottentot and his head seemed altogether too large for
his slender spidery body. His mother successfully
reared him.

child. She received the charge of shot in the back, and came tumbling down through the branches, clutching vainly at them as she fell. We drove off the dogs, and turning to observe her we noticed that she was cowering over her young one, still seeking to protect it with her body. Hugging her baby tight to her breast, she regarded us with a world of sadness in her eyes, and with a gasp and a shudder she died. We forgot for the moment that she was but a monkey, for her actions and expression were so human, that we felt we had committed a crime. Muttering an oath, my friend turned and walked rapidly off, vowing that this was the last time he would shoot a monkey. " It's not sport, it's downright murder," he declared, and I fervently agreed with him.

I have often had Vervet Monkeys in captivity with babies of various ages. When the youngster is very young it clings tenaciously to the breast and side of its mother. Its limbs and body are thin and spidery, and the head is absurdly large for so small and frail-looking a body. Its face is pink and wrinkled, like that of an aged Hottentot, and habitually bears an anxious fretted look. The females are quite friendly when kept together in the same cage, and do not interfere with each other's young ones.

The baby monkey has a curious habit of sucking the two teats of the mother simultaneously. These are sufficiently close together to allow of this. This habit is usually contracted when the youngster begins to find the milk of its parent insufficient for its needs, and probably has some notion it will get more by sucking the two teats at the same time. The mother hugs and nurses the infant in her arms exactly after the manner of a human mother. When climbing a tree she holds it tight to her breast by casting an arm around it ; meanwhile its arms and legs grip her body tight, and each little fist grasps a handful of her fur or skin.

I had one of these apes which gave birth to twins in December 1908. She succeeded in rearing them both. It was most interesting to watch the little mites playing and romping with one another, while the mother looked on approvingly. For the first two months she never permitted them to leave her for a moment ; but as they began to develop they grew playful, and were wishful of exercising their limbs. She could never bear the sight of a dog, and the instant one appeared she would snatch up her children and hug them to her breast, at the same time giving vent to loud threatening cries. From month to month the twins became less dependent upon the mother, and their confidence slowly increased, until eventually they led an existence independent of her ; although, until almost adult, they would rush to her for protection if anything occurred to frighten them.

The Vervet Monkey has a natural antipathy to dogs, and the appearance of one of the latter excites them profoundly. I had two mother monkeys, each of whom had a baby about a month old. One day a friend came to see them, and his terrier dog ran

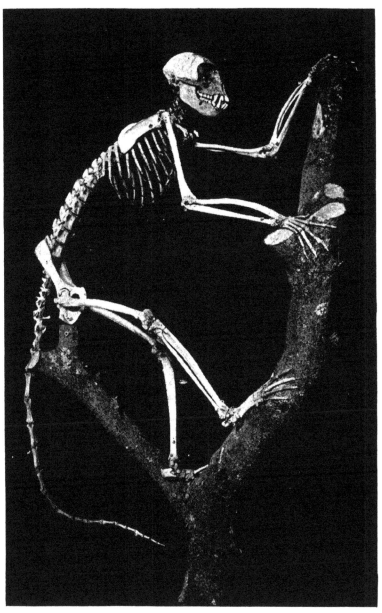

Complete skeleton of a Vervet Monkey or Blaauw-aapje (*Cercopithecus pygerythrus*). (*From a specimen in the Port Elizabeth Museum.*)

forward and barked. Instantly one of the monkeys faced him. Disengaging her baby from her breast, she passed it rapidly over her shoulder to her companion, who was waiting ready to receive it. Snatching it to her breast she, with the two babies held to her breast with one arm, climbed along a thick branch in the cage to the most secure corner. The other, with an expression of anger and defiance on her face, stood ready to do battle, meanwhile giving vent to loud bark-like cries. This loud peculiar cry is only sounded when there is urgent need of help ; and in the wild state, when this cry is heard, the females with their babies flee to the securest retreats, and the others at once bound off to the aid of their comrade in distress. The action of the two mother monkeys referred to was as human-like an act as could be imagined. Both acted in unison for the saving of the children. The moment the one mother faced the dog, the other, instead of also coming to the attack, or else retiring in fear to the inner corner of the cage, instantly ran down the sloping tree trunk to the back of her comrade, took charge of her baby, and attempted to retire to safety, not to save herself, but the lives of the children which she imagined to be in danger.

Vervet Monkeys make interesting exhibits in Zoological Gardens when confined in large airy cages, where they can give full scope to their passion for fun and frolic. They are on the move all day long, and never seem to tire.

Colonists in South Africa often keep one or more of these monkeys chained up to a pole, with a roosting box on top. They make interesting and amusing pets, but their nature is treacherous, and if irritated or annoyed they turn and bite those who feed and pet them. They are very vindictive, and if ill-treated will do their utmost to retaliate. Their teeth are strong and sharp, and the canines are long in fully adult males, and in consequence they are able to inflict nasty wounds. When captured young and kindly treated, they make nice amusing pets until they are about half-grown, when they tend to become untrustworthy and capricious in their temper.

A friend of mine had a pet Vervet for two or three years, and taught it to perform a variety of tricks. I warned him that it would turn on him, but he scoffed at the idea. One day in his absence some mischievous boys teased it dreadfully, working it up into a state almost of frenzy. My friend, unconscious of this, came along shortly after, and the moment he got within reach, the monkey sprang upon his shoulder, and before he could beat it off, the enraged creature had bitten him deeply in the cheek and neck three times.

The wounds suppurated, and healed with difficulty, having to be laid open twice and cauterized. Three months later my friend committed suicide, and left a letter saying that since being bitten by the monkey he had suffered severely from mental depression, which had become intolerable. Absorp-

Forest home of the Vervet Monkeys of South Africa.

tion of the pus from the wounds, no doubt, had induced a lowered condition of health, which brought about this mental derangement.

In the Port Elizabeth Museum I kept a number of live spiders which were on exhibition in glass globes, open at the top. I also had a young Vervet Monkey in a cage adjacent. The latter escaped one day, and before the attendant was aware of the fact it had eaten every one of the spiders. When he appeared it walked up to him and allowed itself to be taken up and put back into its cage, evidently thinking it had rendered us a service in disposing of a score of poisonous insects.

When sleeping, Vervet Monkeys cluster together for warmth in the forks of the branches of great forest trees. Once I startled a number of them from a large cavity at the top of the trunk of a forest tree. On another occasion a score or more were perched on the roof of the nest of a Hammerkop bird (*Scopus umbretta*), and from the interior which had been enlarged. The nests of these birds are sometimes so large that a cart would hardly accommodate one. They are often in trees, and are composed of twigs, sticks, reeds, rushes, &c., with a chamber plastered with mud.

Sometimes these monkeys roost on ledges of rock in sheltered situations. I have never yet met two large troops of monkeys in the same locality. They seem to have their districts as carefully marked out as is the case with us. Should a troop encroach upon the territory of another clan, then war is declared, and the intruders are either driven forth, or the rightful owners are obliged to retreat. These latter sometimes have a bad time, for, in seeking a new home, they are apt to trespass upon the domain of some other troop or clan. Should this latter clan be unable to repel the invaders, they are themselves driven into exile. The history of the monkeyfolk in this respect is exactly similar to that of man.

Should enemies become too numerous, or the food supply prove inadequate, scouts are sent forth to spy out the surrounding country, and should a rich un-occupied district be discovered, the clan migrate to it. If the scouts report a desirable piece of territory occupied by a clan of monkeys small in number, they are attacked, driven forth, and their country seized by the invaders. It is a struggle for the survival of the fittest. The battle goes on with all forms of life, from the lowest kinds of one-celled plants and animals, up to and including man.

Thus do the various forms of life guard against extinction, and at the same time evolve intelligence. The struggle for food and the battling against enemies have been the two forces which have evolved the higher forms of life on our world.

For further information and illustrations about Vervet Monkeys, the reader is referred to my book entitled *The Monkeyfolk of South Africa*, which can be obtained from any bookseller. It is specially written for boys and girls.

Samango Monkey, adult and a young one.

From specimens mounted by F. Teschner.

THE MOSSAMBIQUE VERVET MONKEY
(Cercopithecus pygerythrus rufoviridis)

THE Mossambique Vervet Monkey is a sub-species of the common Vervet or Blue Ape of South Africa. It differs from the latter as follows : the fur of the upper parts has a yellowish shade ; the top of the head, the outer parts of the limbs, and the tail are blackish ; underparts including the inner' sides of the limbs are white instead of having a reddish tinge, as is the case with the typical Vervet.

This sub-species is met with in the north-eastern parts of South Africa. It is common in the Zambesi regions, and in Mossambique. It associates in troops, and its habits are in every way similar to those of the typical species of which it is but a local race.

THE SAMANGO MONKEY
(Cercopithecus labiatus)
Syn.: *C. samango*
Insimango of Amaxosa

THE Samango Monkey inhabits the wooded gorges, kloofs, and dense forests on the eastern side of South Africa, and as far north as the East Coast. It is not by any means plentiful in the eastern parts of the Cape Province or Natal, but is common in the forests of Zululand.

23

The Samango is larger than the Vervet, and darker in colour. A fine male was captured in the King William's Town district a few years ago, and was kept in captivity at the Port Elizabeth Museum.

It was calm, self-possessed, and deliberate in its movements, contrasting strangely with the excitable, nervous, fidgety manner of the Vervet. I introduced a tame Vervet Monkey into its cage, but the Samango instantly attacked it, and we had much difficulty in saving its life. I then caused another cage to be erected next to that of the Samango, with a wire-netting division, and introduced several Vervets into it. The Samango took little or no notice of them after the first day. Six months later the partition was removed, but although the Samango showed no hostility, he took very little notice of the Vervets, and never entered into their games, or allowed himself to in any way become familiar with them. He would sedately sit on a tree trunk and coldly regard their friendly advances. However, he was master in that cage, and the others were well aware of the fact, for they were careful never to attempt to tease or play tricks with him, as they were continually doing with one another. When the daily allowance of food was put into the cage, the Samango satisfied his appetite first, while the others gibbered and looked on longingly, and waited.

One day I scattered fruit over the floor of the cage, and a general scramble ensued amongst the monkeys for it. The Samango bit and cuffed right and left, meanwhile talking in an excited manner in monkey language. Two or three of the Vervets secured some fruit and sprang aloft to the perches with it; but the Samango relentlessly pursued them until they dropped the fruit. With a grunt of satisfaction the pursuer descended to the floor to feed in peace. The second time fruit or nuts were scattered in a similar way, there was the same impulsive rush, but a warning cry from the Samango sent the Vervets in terror back to their perches. After this, a scowl and a grunt were sufficient to intimidate any of the Vervets who attempted to snatch up a morsel of food from the ground, while the aristocratic Samango was dining.

The home of the Samango is in the darkest and gloomiest recesses of the forests, and wooded gorges. In the wild state it never associates with the Vervet, and seldom leaves its secluded leafy retreats; consequently unless driven by desperate hunger it does not interfere with growing crops, except occasionally in Zululand, for instance, where the cultivated fields are adjacent to the forests.

The Zulus prize the skin of the Samango highly. They prepare and convert it into a loin covering, known as Umutsha. Before the annexation of Zululand by the British, the skin of the Samango formed a portion of the distinguishing dress of one of the King's regiments of soldiers; and in order to supply the demand, the Samango was relentlessly hunted and killed.

This species of monkey is not treacherous, excitable, and vindictive like its cousin the typical Vervet; and when captured young it makes an affectionate and gentle pet.

The Samango is somewhat larger than the average Vervet, but the large adult males of the Vervets, such as the leaders of the troops, are quite as big and robust as the Samango. The fur of this monkey is much darker than that of the Vervet, and has a grizzled appearance, owing to each hair being ringed black and yellow; the latter being shorter than the black, the animal, in consequence, at a first glance appears to be blackish in colour. The head is dark, approaching black, but the fur gradually assumes a lighter hue towards the hind parts. The hands and feet are black, forelimbs black, hindlimbs greyish-black. Nails, skin of the inside of the ears, anal callosities, and face black. Tail gradually darkening from the root to the tip.

OTHER SPECIES OF CERCOPITHECUS MONKEYS

THERE is one other species of the genus Cercopithecus and two sub-species, which are included amongst the South African monkeys, but they need not be considered at any length here, as they are all East African species, and are not well known in South Africa, occurring only in the extreme northeast of what is zoologically recognised as South

A Chacma Baboon.

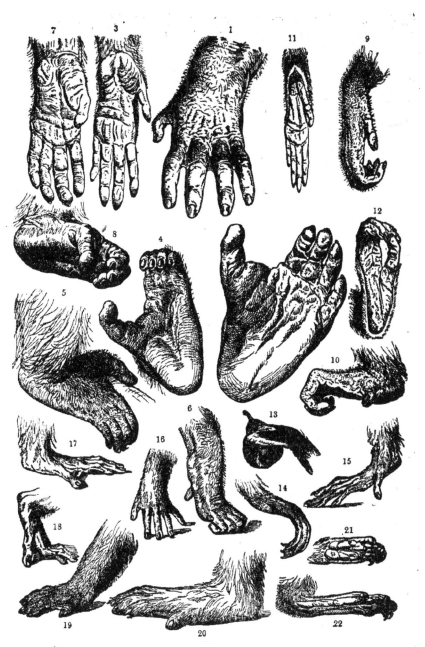

Hands and Feet of Apes and Monkeys.—1, 2, Gorilla; 3–8, Chimpanzee;
9, 10, Orang; 11–13, Gibbon; 14, 15, Guereza; 16–18, Macaque;
19, 20, Baboon; 21, 22, Marmoset.

From " The Royal Natural History " ; Warne & Co., Ltd.

Africa, viz. the country south of the Zambesi and Cunene Rivers.

They are as follows :

THE ZAMBESI MONKEY (*Cercopithecus stairi moss-ambicus*).

SYKES's MONKEY (*Cercopithecus albogularis*), and a sub-species of Sykes's Monkey, viz. *Cercopithecus albogularis beirensis*.

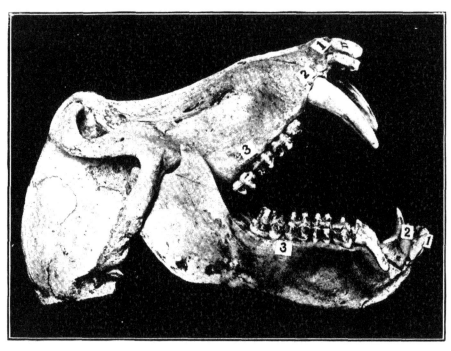

The skull of a male Chacma Baboon, slightly less than one-half natural size.—(1) Incisor or Cutting Teeth; (2) Canine or Tearing Teeth; (3) Molar or Grinding Teeth. The canine or eye teeth are smaller in female Baboons.

THE CAPE BABOON OR BAVIAN

(*Papio porcarius*)

Also known as the Chacma, which is a corruption of the
Hottentot word T'chatikamma; Infene of Amaxosa
(*Stanford*); Imfena of Swazis and Zulus : Tshweni of
Basutos (*Kirby*).

THE Cape Baboon or Bavian inhabits the whole of
South Africa from the Cape to the Zambesi.
Unlike all the species of monkeys of the Vervet
tribe which are strictly arboreal, the baboon is an
inhabitant of the krantzes and bare stony hills ; and
although it can climb trees with facility, yet it
seldom does so except when seeking food in the shape
of wild fruit, berries, seeds, tender leaves, flowers,
and the gum which exudes from the branches of
trees ; or when doing sentry duty for the troop.
However, when krantzes are few, or not steep enough
to afford a secure retreat at night, it sleeps aloft in
tall trees. The Cape Baboon associates in troops
of from a dozen or so to a hundred or more individuals. They are expert rock climbers, and it is
truly a marvellous sight to observe a troop of these
ungainly-looking animals scaling a perpendicular

krantz. They are equally expert in climbing up or down these krantzes.

When chased in rocky country it is quite impossible to follow a troop of baboons, so swiftly do they glide over and amongst the rocks ; and woe betide the dog which ventures after them in their stony retreats.

In Natal I once startled a large troop of baboons, digging up bulbs out upon the flat open ground, some distance from the foot of a krantz which was about a thousand feet in height, and quite perpendicular. The baboons, with loud bark-like cries of alarm, fled. Seeing us starting off in pursuit, the warrior males, about six in number, fell to the rear, glancing every minute or so over their shoulders at us, and barking defiance. Reaching the krantz, the troop swarmed up, and in an incredibly short space of time not a baboon was to be seen. They simply vanished from sight in the face of the precipice. Taking out my field-glasses I carefully scanned the face of the cliff and discovered the reason of this mysterious disappearance. Here and there in the sides of the krantz were cavities, large gaping cracks and ledges. One of these cavities was packed full of baboons, huddled up, and clinging tight to each other like bees. On jutting rocks and ledges, others were flattened out, lying as still as the rocks on which they lay. A big male with shaggy neck was lying hidden in a cavity, the top of his head and eyes alone being visible.

He was carefully watching my movements. I shouted several times, but the baboons paid no heed, evidently thinking they had not been observed. Indeed, without the aid of powerful field-glasses, it would have been quite impossible to have detected a single one of them, so closely did the colour of their fur blend with that of the rocks. I retired to a neighbouring clump of scrub, and hid ; but although I lay low for a full hour, not a baboon stirred. They were awaiting the signal from their leader, who evidently knew perfectly well that I was in hiding, and perhaps with evil intent.

A troop of baboons numbering about 200 of all sizes, from babies in arms to great shaggy-maned males, lived in the crannies and cracks in the perpendicular sides of Table Mountain, near Pietermaritzburg, in Natal. This troop was a pest to the Kafirs living in the vicinity, owing to their frequent raids on the mealie and amabele fields. The natives were in despair, for these sub-human cousins of ours are not easily caught napping.

While a raid on a mealie garden is being carried out, one or more of the troop, as circumstances require, take up a suitable position on a projection of rock, on the top of a pile of boulders, on one of the upper branches of a tall tree, or whatever suitable spot the neighbourhood affords. Should the sentry see or hear anything suspicious, he gives a loud cry of alarm, whereupon the troop instantly rush for their retreat, which in the case of this troop was half way up a cliff a thousand feet in height.

The natives informed us this troop of baboons were in the habit of feeding on the flat top of the mountain during the morning. Three of us led our horses up a steep narrow winding path, and after over an hour's climb we reached the top without mishap. Our Kafir scout had, meanwhile, been reconnoitring, and reported that the baboons were busy digging bulbs in a depression about the centre of the flat-topped mountain. Mounting our horses we rode forth, and gaining the brow of a hillock, we saw a great troop of baboons scattered about, busily engaged digging up bulbs with their fingers. No sentry had been placed on guard on this occasion, for no doubt the baboons thought themselves secure on the top of this great flat-topped table mountain surrounded by perpendicular cliffs.

We had but a momentary glimpse of them in the act of feeding, for on the instant of our appearance over the rise, warning cries rang out, mother apes snatched up their children and the whole troop made off, chattering and screaming. Five large males, in appearance like big broad-shouldered, stunted Kafirs, guarded the rear, ever and anon turning and exposing their great canine teeth, which glittered in the sun. We had double-barrelled guns loaded with loopers, which are the largest kind of shot; and to kill such large and powerful animals as the warrior males, it was neces-

THE CAPE BABOON OR BAVIAN

sary to come to close quarters, so we pressed forward at a gallop. The baboons were making for the edge of the cliff, but were still several hundreds of yards from it when we overtook the troop. Realising the extremity of the danger, the five big males, with loud coughing barks, turned and faced us. In an instant they were joined by a full score of others, also adult, but not so large as the five who were evidently the leaders of the clan. They ranged themselves in a row a few feet apart, and grimly awaited our assault. Our horses were galloping at full speed, and being unable to rein up in time, we swerved to right and left in a semicircle, having no wish to be torn from our saddles and disembowelled. One of our number, whose horse had got out of hand, failed to swerve sufficiently, and as the horse swept past, two of the leaders dashed out to meet him. He fired at random with both barrels, crippling one, and headed his horse at the other, after casting away his gun. The baboon endeavoured to avoid the collision by swerving and at the same time attempting to throw himself on the rider. The horse's shoulder, however, struck the ape with a sickening thud, and next moment the rider, horse, and ape lay in a confused mass on the ground. By this time we had pulled up our horses, dismounted, and were hurrying to the rescue, firing and shouting as we ran. The noise terrified the baboons, for they at once fled, and presently vanished over the edge of the cliff. The one which was wounded also succeeded in gaining the edge and disappeared; but the other which had collided with the horse lay dazed and was killed before it could regain consciousness. Knowing the cliff at this spot was a thousand feet or more in height and quite perpendicular, we felt assured the troop of baboons were lurking amongst the boulders, or the scrubby tufts of bush at the extreme edge of the cliff; so we approached very cautiously, but not a baboon was to be seen. Surely, we thought, the crippled baboon could not have climbed down that terrible krantz, for one of its arms had been broken; but it, too, was gone. Lying flat on our stomachs we peered down that awful precipice, expecting to see some of the baboons still climbing, but all was still—every ape had vanished.

We acknowledged ourselves beaten—yes, badly beaten. The horse had broken its neck, and our friend lay stunned and covered with cuts and bruises.

On another occasion a farmer friend in Natal, who had been driven to desperation by the raids of a troop of baboons on his crops, organised a hunt. There were several of us mounted, including three Kafirs on absurdly small, but tough and wiry ponies. We had planned to cut off the troop from their sanctuary, but failed.

We essayed to run them down before they could reach the edge of a krantz for which they were making. One of the Kafirs, who had galloped some distance ahead of us, and who was brandishing his gun in

A youngster of the Baboonfolk eating a banana.

the air and shouting excitedly, failed to hear our shouts of warning, or else his pony had got out of hand. Anyway, as we were reining up we saw him dash headlong amongst the baboons and heard the report of his gun, and a moment later both he and his pony shot out into space over the edge of the krantz and were smashed upon the rocks in the gorge far below.

Within a few yards of the bodies of man and horse, the dead body of a large male baboon was found. It was evident the ape had come in contact with the horse at the edge of the cliff and been hurled over ; but whether it was accidentally ridden into or had sought to bar the way we knew not, as our attention at the time had been concentrated on the horse and its rider rushing to what we knew was certain death.

One day the overseer of a farm in the Graaff Reinet district went to the veld, leaving the bottom half of the door of his cottage bolted, and the top half open. During his absence a troop of baboons came from the mountain, and, with characteristic curiosity, examined the premises, and finally began hopping over the half-door into the house. At this stage it is presumed some old " mannetje," more clumsy than the rest, must have slammed to the upper half, or perhaps it was the wind. Anyway, twelve or fifteen baboons suddenly found themselves shut up in the house, and then the trouble began. In leaping up the walls in their terror and excitement they completely wrecked the interior, tore things down, broke and smashed the household goods, and, as baboons will do, made a very disgusting mess about the place. In the end one of them must have jumped against the window and smashed the glass, and the whole lot got out and returned to the krantzes.

The diet of the baboon is, as a general rule, poor and by no means too plentiful. In fact, in some of the dry stony districts inhabited by troops of these animals, it is a matter for surprise how they are able to procure sufficient for their needs. The diet consists of bulbs and roots which they scrape up out of the ground with their strong finger-nails. This is supplemented by sweet bark, the white pith of aloe stems, tender shoots, buds, flowers, wild fruits, berries, seeds, and the gum which oozes from acacia trees. In the parts where the prickly pear abounds, the fruit forms a welcome addition to the baboons' diet. A variety of insect life is also devoured, such as scorpions, spiders, millipedes, beetles, centipedes, &c., which are usually found under loose stones lying on the hillsides. It is a common sight to see a troop of baboons busily turning over the stones in search of the various insects which find shelter beneath. There is an amusing story of a coleopterist, commonly miscalled a "bug-hunter," who had recently arrived in the country. Being informed that a certain stony hillside was a good hunting-ground for beetles, he forthwith set out. On arrival at the place, eager to begin operations, he found that nearly every loose stone on the hillside had recently been turned over, and went off highly disgusted, thinking that a rival coleopterist had forestalled him.

Baboons are exceedingly fond of honey, and the larvæ or bee grubs in the comb, and will risk getting stung by the angry bees to obtain this much-coveted dainty. Should a bees' nest be located in the hollow interior of an old branch, tree trunk, or in a hole in the ground or rock crevice, an opening large enough for the withdrawal of the comb is made by scratching with the finger-nails. The arm is then thrust in, a piece of comb pulled out, and the robber makes off, dragging the honeycomb through the foliage as he runs, or rubbing it on the grass to dislodge any bees which might be clinging to it. Plunging into the thick scrub where the infuriated bees cannot follow, he devours the choice morsel at his leisure. When the bees have calmed down, he makes a second rush, dives his hand into the hole, grabs another lump of comb, and again bolts for shelter. When the comb contains bee grubs, these are extracted from their cells with the finger and thumb, one by one, in a most deliberate and painstaking manner. These attacks on bee-hives are usually carried out early in the morning before sunrise when the air is chilly and the bees, in consequence, more or less lethargic. Except in those districts where the rainfall is regular and abundant, the natural diet of the baboon is none too plentiful, and these animals are often driven almost to desperation by hunger, and it is little matter for wonder they take to raiding the crops and orchards of the farmers and aborigines. Once they get a taste of the produce of the farmer, they are loth to return to their former meagre fare. So they continue to raid the cultivated fields, planning their raids with the greatest of care and cunning. The exasperated farmer eventually, in self-defence, gathers together a party of neighbours and friends, and in the dead of night surrounds the retreat of the baboons. At break of day the attack is made, and if well planned, sometimes an entire troop is annihilated. So wholesale a slaughter, however, seldom occurs, for the baboons are exceedingly cunning, and the greater proportion of them usually succeed in stealing off and escaping unobserved. However, so cunning are these apes that they invariably take up their abode in a retreat which is either impossible or difficult to surround.

We were once completely outwitted by a troop of baboons in Natal. A Hottentot had located their retreat in the face of a krantz, near the foot of which, at some little distance, was a forest. A large party of us completely surrounded the krantz, and waited for daylight. The darkness was lightened by the feeble rays of a young moon, and the baboons unfortunately either saw us, or becoming suspicious, a scout was sent out to investigate, for they began barking. They continued to bark for some time, but eventually ceased, and all was silent, save the occasional cry of some night animal or bird in the adjacent forest.

Grimly we waited for daylight, to annihilate this troop of baboons which had for two years or more been raiding the cultivated fields in the neighbourhood. On the first appearance of dawn we carefully watched for some signs of the baboons, knowing too well their cunning and crafty nature, but all was still—not a movement amongst the rocks in the face of the krantz could we see.

When the light grew strong we, who were below, fired a volley at the rocks ; and from the tangled, thorny undergrowth in the midst of the forest at the back of us, the baboons barked derisively. Yes, we had been out-generalled. The baboons, under cover of darkness, had actually stolen past us through the grass and escaped into the forest, which offered a perfect sanctuary, at least from us. The baboons must have crept past us in single file, for we were standing on guard, each beside his horse, within fifty paces of one another.

Pressed by hunger, the baboons have of late taken to stealing ostrich eggs. They break the shells by banging the eggs against each other, or on a stone. I saw a baboon take up an ostrich egg and carry it to a small boulder and drop it upon the stone. It was careful not to cast it violently down, knowing that if the shell was badly smashed, the contents would escape. The egg, in this instance, was slightly dented. Taking it up, the baboon carefully picked out the broken bits of shell, and proceeded to suck out the contents.

Another evil habit which some of the baboons have acquired, is to capture young lambs and kids, which they kill and disembowel to get at the stomach, which is torn open for the sake of the curdled milk it usually contains, and of which the baboons are very fond. How they learned there was milk in the stomachs of lambs, and kids, we can but conjecture. Needless to say, these habits have considerably increased the enmity of the farmers against them.

In spite of the most determined efforts of man to destroy the baboons, they still exist in considerable numbers. Many troops of them have altered their habits, and have sought sanctuary in the recesses of the dense thorny forests, wooded kloofs, and valleys, where they are safe from pursuit by man. From these retreats they issue forth, but are careful never to venture far from the edge of their leafy cover.

In consequence of this comparative immunity from their arch-enemy—Man, they multiply unduly, and the balance of Nature is upset, for food becomes increasingly scarce. Driven to desperation by hunger, they lose their dread of their human foe in their dire necessity, and boldly issue forth and raid his fields, with the inevitable result that sooner or later their numbers are considerably reduced by the angry farmers.

THE CAPE BABOON OR BAVIAN

Baboons are not without some redeeming qualities as far as man is concerned. The migratory locust levies a heavy toll on the produce of the farmer, besides eating off the natural vegetation on which stock animals subsist. Notwithstanding the continuous efforts of the Government to exterminate these vast swarms of locusts, they still exist, and the slightest laxity in the prosecution of the warfare against them results in fresh swarms breeding out and devastating the country. The baboon is extremely fond of locusts, and devours them with avidity. I have seen troops of baboons swarm down from their rocky fastnesses and remain the entire day out on the veld, capturing and eating these insect pests. The Vervet Monkeys also wage war on the swarms of locusts when they come to roost on the tree-tops in the early evening, or during the early morning, when, owing to the coldness of the air, they are unable to fly.

Baboons seem to know the difference between a European with a gun, and a Kafir with assegais or kerries. In Natal I always noticed they made off to their retreats long before we could get within range, even of a rifle. It was quite evident they possessed keen and long-distance vision—practically telescopic.

Whenever I wandered about unarmed, the baboons allowed me to approach within fifty yards. One day I stood at the foot of a stony hill watching a troop of baboons sunning themselves on the rocks. A large male was keeping me under observation all the time; but considering me an inoffensive sort of person he was not alarmed, and the other members of the troop sprawled on the rocks or played practical jokes with one another. They were quite satisfied that if there was any danger, or even the slightest suspicion of it, their leader would give the alarm. Suddenly I pulled a pair of field-glasses from my pocket and applied them to my eyes. On the instant the old male baboon gave a succession of warning grunts and barks, and every baboon of the troop vanished from sight behind boulders or into crevices in the rocks. Watching closely I saw a score or more of baboons peering at me over the top or round the corners of boulders, their eyes and eyebrows alone being visible. They remained hidden until I retired to some distance. The field-glasses were new to them, and they, no doubt, suggested something of the nature of a firearm.

The Kafirs in Natal are not allowed to possess firearms, except in the case of a privileged few, and the baboons knew this perfectly well—they didn't know of the Government regulation, but they knew a Kafir rarely carried a firearm. So taking advantage of this fact they used to invade the Kafirs' mealie and amabele fields in the boldest manner; and when the natives turned out with their dogs, the baboons would sullenly retire, the warriors of the troop falling to the rear and barking threateningly as they retreated. Sometimes when the men were absent, the women would turn out, and with shouts and yells, and the waving of blankets, endeavour to drive off the robbers. In these instances, although they always retreated, yet they did so in a very leisurely manner, and if a dog was bold enough to attempt to come to close quarters it quickly lost its life.

It does not take the baboons long to find out that there is little or nothing to fear from native women, whose only weapons are their tongues.

Advantage was taken of this fact by a farmer acquaintance of mine. It seems when he and his two sons rode forth to superintend operations on distant portions of the farm, the baboons from some neighbouring wooded krantzes took advantage of the fact to rob the orchard, which was some little distance from the homestead. ' They heeded not the cries of the lady of the house and her two Hottentot women servants. In fact after a time they became quite threatening in their demeanour, and actually chased the women. A trap was laid. The farmer and his two sons dressed themselves in the women's clothes, and the women donned the men's attire and rode away. After about half an hour the troop of baboons came scrambling down from their rocky retreat. The three men, who had their breech-loading guns concealed in the folds of their ample skirts, advanced, shouting shrilly, and casting stones after the manner of women. Getting within short range, the three opened fire, selecting the big shaggy males. There was no more orchard-raiding by that troop of baboons.

Once I rode in the rear of a party of Zulus who, with a pack of mongrel dogs, were on their way to endeavour to cut off a troop of baboons on a neighbouring hillside. Some of the dogs, scenting the baboons, became excited and rushed from the cover of the scrub, under shelter of which it was hoped the baboons could have been approached and cut off from their retreat. The natives, with hoarse yells of execration, tried to run down the baboons. Some of the dogs lost all sense of caution in their excitement, and rushed ahead at the retreating troop. Four big hairy male baboons immediately fell to the rear, retreating slowly. When the dogs were within a few paces of them they, with one accord, swung round and each seized a dog. It was all done so rapidly, systematically, and withal so cunningly, that the dogs were taken quite by surprise. I saw the victims partially raised from the ground, then gripped with the terrible dagger-like fangs, and next instant they were impotently kicking and struggling on the ground. All this took but a few seconds of time, and before the other dogs had come to close quarters, the baboons had made off and joined the troop. Once again they made a stand, but the remaining dogs were too wary to be caught, and contented themselves by barking furiously. Retreating with short quick rushes, and turning at intervals to intimidate their canine pursuers, the baboons eventually reached the dense thorny scrub and vanished.

The baboon does not bite after the manner of most other animals. The victim is gripped with the hands, the great canine teeth are driven home in the flesh, and with a tremendous heave the body of the victim is thrust away from the jaws, the sharp-edged canine teeth cutting through the flesh like a knife. These teeth are specially evolved for the purpose, the cutting edge being at the back.

I once saw a wounded male baboon pick up a pointer dog, and with a single bite completely rip open its abdomen, so that its bowels protruded. These warrior males are terrible antagonists when brought to bay, and an unarmed man in the grip of one stands no chance of victory, for if his throat is not immediately torn out, he would soon be otherwise crippled.

In Natal our assistance was once solicited by some natives who were actually being terrorised by a troop of baboons. It seems the only available water supply was from a spring in a kloof, the sides of which were strewn with boulders and covered more or less by a tangled mass of vegetation, largely of a thorny nature. The native girls and women are the carriers of water, the men considering it beneath their dignity to do so.

Baboons are well aware that native women do not carry weapons, and that they are not to be feared overmuch. At first the troop used to stand on some neighbouring boulders and bark threateningly. Becoming bolder after a time, they drew nearer, but were intimidated by the women casting stones at them. One day, however, they became very threatening, and barking loudly to keep up their courage, they advanced. The women fled screaming, leaving their calabashes and earthenware water-vessels behind. The baboons contented themselves with smashing the utensils.

On the following day they were bolder and advanced from their rocky retreat the moment the women appeared. After this it was necessary for the women to be escorted by some men armed with kerries and assegais. Sometimes boys did escort duty. The baboons realising their little game was up, retired high up the hill and barked. This escorting of the women became irksome, and a strong desire to wipe out the Imfena, as they termed the baboons, took possession of them. On inspection of the locality we came to the conclusion that nothing short of shelling the bush with artillery would dislodge them. We taught those interfering baboons a lesson, however. Creeping up under cover before daylight, we lay hidden until sunrise, which was the time agreed upon for the women to come to the spring for water. Talking and laughing loudly to attract the attention of the baboons, they approached the water ; but like spectres, the entire troop of baboons appeared upon the boulders which jutted out from the tangled masses of vegeta-

A typical South African krantz, which some people call a precipice.
Such places are the homes of the Baboonfolk.

tion. Chattering and barking, they advanced, led by three great deep-chested, long-maned males. One of the three, we noticed, was unusually large and powerful, and was, from his bold bearing, the commander-in-chief, the other two being, no doubt, his captains. The women pretending to be terribly afraid, screamed and gesticulated, and when the troop had approached within about fifty yards they fled, leaving their water-vessels. The baboons set up a curious grunting noise, and advanced more rapidly. Presently they gathered round the small pool like a lot of children, chattering and gibbering excitedly, while some of their number were attempting to secure the calabashes which were floating on the water. Singling out the leaders, we took careful aim and fired at their heads. We had double-barrelled breech-loading shot guns loaded with the largest calibre of shot known as "loopers." Both the baboons sank down with shattered skulls. Quick as thought both of us fired at the third warrior male, and he too sank down dead. Before we could reload the troop had vanished. In any case we had no intention of shooting at them. They had been taught a lesson which they would never forget. Although this troop of baboons continued to inhabit the kloof they never again molested the women, nor did they again raid the adjacent fields.

A wonderful migration of baboons took place during August of 1914, on the Ceres side of the Mitchells Pass Mountains, in the Cape Province.

Their caves and other mountain retreats on the west had presumably been rendered untenable by furious and continuous storms, there being torrential rain and snow mixed, and a great gale blowing for three consecutive days. Whilst the railway workers were watching the subsidences at Varney's Corner, a big black mass of jumping, barking, howling baboons were seen coming down the mountains not far away. They were fully 500 in number—a moderate estimate—and, young and old, they came leaping down across the railway and divisional road, and were seen to make their way to the river bed, just then filled with a very violent foaming torrent.

They made their way to what was apparently known to them to be a safe crossing, because here the tops of some big rocks in the stream were just clear above the boiling water, and then they called a halt. One big Jack was seen to make the attempt, and he evidently was aware of the risk even to that class of animal, accustomed to flying leaps, and he got safely across the river, which was now very wide there. Then another and another of the males made a successful attempt, not one missing its footing, although the leap at one or two points was very wide.

Now a remarkable scene was to follow: the youngsters could not possibly make this leap unassisted, and the mothers took them up and carried them with them in this formidable jump. Some were held under their arms, some on their backs,

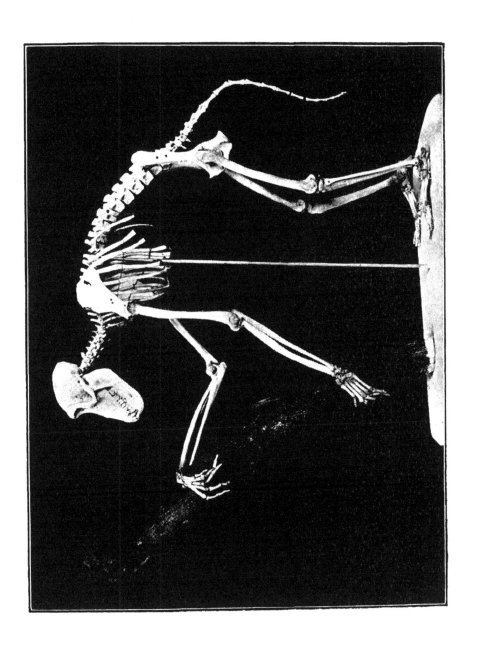

and in this way they succeeded in crossing the turbid stream. If the Jacks had a big task, that of the mothers with the youngsters on their backs was still greater. The little army of baboons was so long getting over this one crossing that the river had visibly increased in volume before they were all over. The last to get across had a most precarious time of it, as their jumping-stones were now under water.

When the last of the big baboons had got over, it was seen that two youngsters had been left behind. These could neither join the army across the flood, nor could their seniors return to assist them. When this was noted by the army leaders, a tremendous noisy, barking, chattering din was set up, in which the youngsters on the other side plaintively joined. This was maintained for some time, when the army dwindled away in the semi-darkness up the kloof at the back of the Castle Mountains. The two deserted youngsters stayed for a while longer at the brink, and then slowly retraced their steps the way they had come from the west.

The educated traveller in the Cape Province is astonished to see the Cactus plant, commonly known as the Prickly Pear, growing abundantly on the stony hills and rocky slopes of the valleys, and wonders how it got there. This cactus plant was introduced from Mexico into South Africa by the Voortrekker Dutch, owing to its usefulness in fence making. It was also planted round the cattle and sheep kraals

to keep carnivorous wild animals from preying on
the stock, for the thick mass of prickly pear presents
an effectual barrier to the larger carnivora, such as
wild dogs, hyænas, jackals, leopards, and lions.
Some of the Voortrekkers planted great broad hedges
of this prickly pear round one or more of their stone
barns, and when threatened with an attack from the
warlike Kafirs, the family, with the servants, retired
into this retreat, the entrance being barricaded with
a wagon or two, around and under which the thorny
branches of the mimosa tree were thrust and secured.
From the loft of the barn the cattle and sheep kraals,
as well as the dwelling-house, could be commanded.
The only weapons in those days were flint-lock guns,
which were loaded, as a rule, with heavy-calibre shot,
or bits of lead cut in small squares and known as
" slugs." With these the resolute and hardy
pioneers of South African civilisation beat off the
attacks of bloodthirsty native hordes.

The prickly pear bears a fruit which is good and
wholesome, and the baboons were not long in finding
this out. Unfortunately the seeds pass through the
alimentary canal unchanged, and in consequence
the rocky fastnesses inhabited by the baboons
were soon covered with masses of prickly pear
bush. In some places the stony slopes of hills
are so covered with prickly pear as to be practically impenetrable.

Although on level ground the baboon can easily
be overtaken by dogs, yet on the stony slopes of

A Baboon Warrior's Weapons.—(1) Upper Canine or Eye Tooth,
two inches long, not including the part in the socket of the
jaw. The back edge of the tooth is as sharp as a knife blade.
(2) Ditto showing the deep groove or channel down the front
of the tooth. (3 and 4) The Lower Canine Teeth.

hills, or in rocky bush-covered localities, they can outdistance any dog.

I was with a party of Dutch friends in Natal who were on their way to a distant kloof where a leopard had been located. On turning the corner of a hill several long-drawn-out, hoarse barks rang out from a baboon perched on a pinnacle of rock. In response to the warning cries, a troop of baboons which had been busily engaged digging up bulbs on the veld, made with the greatest haste for an adjacent stony hill. The dogs of our party gave chase, and we followed as fast as the uneven nature of the ground would permit a horse to travel. The baboons reached the foot of the hill safely, and scattered among the boulders. Three of the dogs foolishly followed, and when almost out of breath with the unusual exertion of running uphill amongst a mass of boulders and loose stones, they were set upon by the leaders of the baboon troop. On our arrival some little time later one dog was found to be disembowelled, another's thigh was torn to shreds, and a third had a horrible wound on his shoulder.

On another occasion in a similar situation on a stony hillside we arrived just in time to save a small pack of Kafir dogs from death. The baboons were retreating up the hill, followed by the dogs. They were evidently luring the dogs on. Suddenly about half of the troop of baboons turned and endeavoured to surround the dogs. The baboons which continued to retreat were the females with youngsters. However, as they began closing in on the now terrified dogs, we happened to arrive, and a few shots from our rifles sent them off up the hill again. It is usually young or inexperienced dogs which fall victims to baboons. Dogs which have hunted baboons, and have come to close quarters with them, and escaped with their lives, learn how to make the attack with the best chance of coming off best. They learn that the baboon always seeks to grip his antagonist before biting, and, by keeping out of arms' length, and circling round and round the baboon, they daze and frighten him. Their object is to keep him at bay until the arrival of their master. Should the baboon attempt to retreat, he is at a disadvantage, for the dogs instantly attack him from behind. I saw a splendid fight put up by a warrior baboon. He was overtaken by a number of dogs. He might easily have escaped with the troop, but the fine old fellow, thinking the youngsters were in danger of being overtaken by the dogs before they could gain a place of safety, turned and engaged the dogs in combat. A greyhound in advance of the rest attacked him and was killed within a moment or two. When we arrived the baboon was facing the howling pack of dogs with his back to a bit of rock, and the lines

> " Come one, come all, this rock shall fly
> From its firm base as soon as I "

immediately occurred to me.

Leaves of the Prickly Pear, showing the fruit on which the
Baboons greedily feed.

THE CAPE BABOON OR BAVIAN

Did I shoot him? No! a thousand times no! I stoned off the dogs and left him in peace. In my rambles over mountain, veld, and in forest, I have met with more examples of the truest heroism and absolute self-sacrifice amongst the lower animals than I have with the higher animal known as Man.

A Dutch farmer near Graaff Reinet possessed a large and powerful dog of the boarhound breed, which was a veteran at baboon-hunting. When a female or immature baboon was overtaken he simply dashed headlong at it, and usually succeeded in killing it without much injury to himself. He never, however, came at once to close quarters with a baboon leader. He baited it for some time, when, getting it at a disadvantage, he would close with it. If the baboon was an exceptionally large one, he would keep it at bay till the arrival of his master. Should the baboon turn and retreat, it was instantly bitten in the loins or back legs. Sometimes he would make an oblique dash at the retreating baboon, gashing its side with a side stroke of his fangs, usually in the abdominal region. This old canine baboon-slayer was covered with scars of former battles. One of these scars was a foot and a half long. A baboon had managed to get a grip of him, and ripped a great patch of skin from his shoulder. Fortunately the skin was not entirely detached, and after treatment with antiseptics it was stitched in place and soon healed up.

Attempts have been made to destroy baboons

with various kinds of poison, but with comparatively little success, for the reason that these animals, and in fact all the monkey tribe, have acute senses of taste and smell; and being of a highly suspicious nature, they refuse to touch even their favourite foods should they detect anything strange in the taste or smell of them.

A friend who wished to destroy an old captive baboon which had become morose and vicious, tried several well-known poisons, one of which was a tasteless preparation of morphia; yet the baboon, although famishing with hunger, refused them one and all, in spite of the poison having been cunningly introduced into choice and dainty ripe fruits.

A farmer succeeded in poisoning several of a troop of baboons in a rather curious and ingenious way.

Finding they resorted to a certain belt of mimosa trees to feed on the gum which oozed from the branches and trunks, he paid a visit to the spot, and, with a penknife, made slits in the soft gum and introduced wax pellets containing strychnine, carefully closing up the cuts and singeing them to destroy the smell left by his fingers. However, the baboons became suspicious after several of their number had died in convulsions, and others fell sick after having eaten freely of the gum; and, connecting it with the death and sickness of their comrades, they never again returned to that locality.

Tame baboons are sometimes used by travellers in the drier districts of South Africa to locate edible

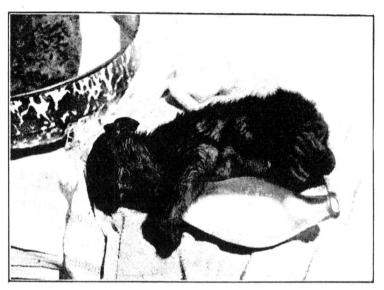

This is Billy the orphan Baboon having his breakfast after his bath, while the sun is drying his coat.

Billy has a nap after breakfast.

When he is cosy and warm and his stomach is full, he has a nap for an hour or so. Even in his sleep he clings tenaciously to his dearly beloved bottle.

bulbs underground. These bulbs are reservoirs of water, but some of them are poisonous. So acute are the senses of taste and smell of the baboons, that it is perfectly safe to eat anything of which one of these apes partakes. The presence of water beneath the surface of the ground is also discovered at times by means of a baboon. The animal is given some salty food, and water is withheld until the poor creature is almost mad with thirst. It is then led out on a cord, long enough to allow it sufficient freedom to range to right and left. Should water be within a few feet of the surface, the baboon at once detects its presence, and begins digging with its fingers. Spades are procured and a hole is sunk. This plan is often very successful in the dry beds of rivers, or in hollows or other situations where water accumulates after a sudden downfall of rain. The water soaks through the sandy surface and gathers on a stratum of clay, through which it cannot soak; and although the surface may at the time be dry and baked, yet within perhaps three feet of the surface there is a considerable quantity of water available if a hole is dug, for the water at once begins to drain into this hole, and may be ladled out.

The Cape Baboon, when young, makes one of the most affectionate and loving of pets, and is lively, playful, and free from malice. When it becomes adult, however, it loses its playfulness, and frequently gets surly and morose, and cannot always be trusted. I have seen serious injury done to people by tame adult baboons. I have seen them, when teased, provoked in other ways, or scolded, suddenly attack their owners, and inflict dreadful bites. On the contrary, I have known adult baboons which have been kept in captivity for years to be docile and affectionate, and their owners assured me they were free from vice.

It is indeed no wonder captive baboons usually become irritable, surly, and untrustworthy, for the life of the average captive baboon is not by any means a happy one.

Doomed to pass its existence secured by a chain a yard or two in length, half-starved, wrongly fed or over-fed, the captive baboon is petted and teased by turn; practical jokes are played off on it; boys are allowed to stone it, and in sundry ways it is tormented. Unscientifically fed, and its evil instincts rendered abnormal, can it be blamed for turning and rending its persecutors ?

The female baboon has only one baby at a birth. I have known two instances of twins, but this, as with other species of the monkey folk, is unusual.

A troop of baboons were surprised when raiding a mealie field, and all but one got safely away to their stony, inaccessible retreat. When my friend and his two sons, who were giving chase on horseback, began to gain on the laggard, two males were seen to leave the troop and linger, and it was apparent they were waiting for their comrade. However, seeing the horsemen coming straight on, they became terrified, and fled. When the pursuers were reining up to shoot, the baboon which could not manage to keep pace with the troop faced round and set up a series of piteous screams and barks. The reason for its inability to keep up with its fellows became apparent, for clinging to its side and breast were two babies, whose faces wore an expression of terror. The farmer, who had been exasperated by repeated raids on his crops, with an oath raised his gun to shoot, but, divining his intention, the mother baboon turned her back to him, and at the same time threw her arms round her children and crouched over them. She received the charge of shot in her lungs, and fell forward, her last effort being to thrust her babies under her body. The two youngsters were subsequently given to me, and were reared. For the first two months they were fed on cows' milk, diluted one-third with water, and a little lime water added. They sucked this readily from an Allenbury baby's feeding-bottle. They had a bottle each to prevent them squabbling, for, should one be fed before the other, the lamentations it set up were loud, piteous, and long. The little fellow thought itself very badly treated, and said so in his own peculiar way.

We established peace and harmony by handing the bottles of milk simultaneously to the two. Hugging the bottles tightly, they retired to their respective corners, looking now and then fearfully over their shoulders; then, pushing the teat of the bottle into the mouth, the milk was greedily sucked up. When the bottles were emptied of their contents, they were at once abandoned, and no further notice was taken of them.

The baby baboon is as human in its ways as any human child, and has the advantage of being more amusing.

A European woman of the illiterate class, the wife of a drayman at North End, Port Elizabeth, lost her baby when it was a few days old. She developed what is commonly known as "milk fever," and a neighbour induced her to nurse a little mite of a baboon which had been found clinging to its mother's breast after she had been shot when in the act of helping herself to some fruit in an orchard. For months this woman suckled the baby baboon, and when I saw the little fellow he was robust and chubby and full of fun. The instant a stranger approached he, with cries of alarm, rushed to his foster-mother, climbed up her dress, and clung to her neck, looking over his shoulder with a comical expression of fear on his face. I asked the woman, in jest, if she would sell him to me, whereupon gleams of fierce anger shot from her eyes, her face hardened, and she, with an oath, ejaculated, "Sell my little darling! No, never!— not for a thousand pounds."

The chief natural enemy of the baboon in the past in South Africa was the leopard. Stealing unobserved upon a troop of baboons, the leopard

Baboon Twins.

(*a*) The twins. One of them is showing jealousy because her
brother got his supper first.

(*b*) The twins posing for their photograph.

seizes a female, or a young one, and at once makes off with it into the undergrowth. Should a troop of baboons be fortunate enough to find a retreat in the face of a krantz, they are safe from their dreaded enemy during the hours of darkness; but if they are compelled to sleep in trees or in rocky or other situations to which the leopard can climb, then a heavy toll is levied on the troop. The baboon, like ourselves, cannot see well at night, and, when attacked at these times, becomes nervous and excited. When a leopard establishes himself near the retreat of a troop of baboons, the latter retire to some distant situation, if such is obtainable, they knowing that otherwise an almost daily toll will be levied upon them, until the entire troop is annihilated.

A leopard will rarely attempt to attack one of the leaders of a troop of baboons, knowing that these shaggy old fellows have great strength and formidable fangs. Should a leopard seize a young baboon during the daytime, he must be quick in seeking cover amidst the tangled thorny scrub, otherwise he will have the enraged troop upon him, and then his time is short, for the males rush at him in a body and tear him to ribbons.

A friend was endeavouring to stalk a troop of baboons which were basking in the sun on some boulders on a stony hillside sparsely covered with stunted scrubby bush. He, however, was not the only stalker. He was in the act of peering through a bush when an agonising succession of shrieks and squeals rent the air. In an instant there was an uproar amongst the baboons, and, with one accord, every male member of the troop rushed in the direction of the noise. A leopard had stalked a female baboon and seized her. She clutched a bush and clung on for dear life, and the leopard, seeing the imminent danger he was in, let go his hold and fled, pursued by the yelling, barking crowd of angry baboons. My friend did not wait to see the result of the chase, but crept off as rapidly as possible, fearing lest the enraged troop might detect his presence and attack him.

The leopards are being rapidly shot off in South Africa by hunters and the pioneer farmers ; and, except in Rhodesia, the baboon has comparatively little to fear from them.

In the past the Chita, or Hunting Leopard, harried the baboons considerably, but he too is vanishing from South Africa. The arch-enemy of the baboon is Man. That this interesting ape, which is so human in its ways, should have to be destroyed seems a pity, but sentiment cannot be permitted to bar the way to the population of the earth by the superior animal—Man. It would be a thousand pities, however, if the Cape Baboon, which is so typical of our country, should be allowed to become extinct. No doubt at some future time reserves will be established in which it may lead a peaceful, harmless existence.

An old pointsman at Uitenhage, who had lost his

legs, and who had wooden substitutes, was employed
as a signalman on the railway. He had a tame baboon
which he taught not only to know each lever by
name, but to pull them as required, and push them
back into position when the train had passed. He
had only to call out the name of the lever, and the
baboon instantly pulled it. When the day's work
was over the ape helped his master to put his light
travelling trolley on the line, and actually pushed
it up the inclines. It was most amusing to watch
the baboon strenuously pushing the man on the
trolley along the line, and to observe how eagerly
and joyously it took its seat on the back of the
trolley on a down grade when it skimmed along
by its own weight.

The story of this baboon is most interesting, and
deserves to be placed on record. He was known
by sight to nearly all the residents of Port Elizabeth;
and the Uitenhagers were so proud of their sub-
human cousin's cleverness that his history and
exploits were told to friends and acquaintances far
and wide. A railway guard named James Edwin
Wide was knocked down by a train in 1877, and both
legs were severed at the knees. He was subsequently
given the job of gatekeeper, and afterwards promoted
to signalman. Wide's cottage was some distance
from the signal-box, and finding it not only hard
but slow work journeying to and fro on his wooden
pegs, he made a light trolley for himself. One day
he saw a half-grown baboon on the market and

bought him. Jack was taught by his master to work the levers of the signals, and, in fact, to be handy in a variety of ways. It was one of Wide's duties to keep the key of the padlock which locked a pair of points off the Graaff Reinet line which led to the coal-yard. When an engine-driver came down for coal the customary signal of four whistles was blown, whereupon Wide went into the signal-box and, taking the key from a nail on the wall, he handed it to the driver as he slowly steamed past the platform. On his return the driver whistled again, and the key was taken from him by Wide, who stood ready to grasp it as the engine passed. The baboon, who answered to the name of Jack, anticipated his master one day, and, taking the key from the nail, he handed it to the driver himself, and, waiting until he returned, Jack took the key again and replaced it on the nail. His master showed his pleasure by fondling and praising him. Never again had Wide occasion to perform this duty. The instant the four whistles sounded, Jack raced for the key, to obtain which he always placed one hand on top of the closed half-door to raise himself sufficiently to get it. He always gripped the same spot, and the wood in course of time became worn down.

Jack was up early, and began the day by carrying water and performing various household duties. The lonely signalman and Jack partook of an early breakfast together, and then set off to work. Jack

Jack and his master about to depart for home after a tiring day's work.

adjusted the trolley on the line himself by getting behind it and pushing it until the front wheels came in contact with the rails. Then, sitting on his haunches, he threw the wheels over the rail, and, taking hold of the trolley, he, by a skilful combination of dexterity and strength, gave a twist and a push, and, behold ! the wheels were on the rails. Wide having taken his seat on the front of the trolley, with his wooden pegs sticking straight out, Jack gripped the back of the vehicle and pushed it along to the signal-box. Without help he threw it off the line and pushed it up against the side of the platform on which the signal cabin stood. Before Jack's advent, Wide employed a big mongrel dog to pull the trolley. When Jack came on the scene and was instructed in his various duties, Wide continued to use the dog, which was harnessed to the trolley, and Jack assisted by pulling from a chain. One end of this chain was attached to a leather band around Jack's loins, and the other end was fastened to a hook on one of Wide's wooden legs. The dog was killed by a passing train, and for many years Jack took his master to and fro unaided. After the dog's death Jack discovered it was easier to push than to pull the trolley along. He gripped the railway metal with his feet, and used his forelimbs for pushing.

Arrived at the box, Wide and Jack at once settled down to work. A whistle is heard, and Jack springs to the " home " signal lever, his master taking the

" distant " one. The train past, Jack mutely pulls back the lever. Jack knew every one of the various signals, and which lever to pull, as well as his master did himself. Mr Geo. B. Howe, writing in the year 1890, after a visit to Jack, said : " It was very touching to see his fondness for his master. As I drew near they were both sitting on the trolley, one of the baboon's arms around his master's neck, the other stroking his face. At my approach Jack jumped to the ground, but his strong love could not be restrained : now he was stroking Wide's face, then his hand, then, with a touch as light as a woman's, brushing a speck of dust off his master's trousers, and the while keeping up an incessant chatter."

One day his master, crossing the line to take a stone out of the points, fell and hurt his arm, and Jack took over all his master's duties until he recovered.

The work was by no means light. Off and on all day the levers were worked. Jack stood 4 ft. 6 in. in height, and his strength was so great that he pulled the distant signal, which was three-quarters of a mile off, with ease. Work over, Jack placed the trolley on the line and pushed his master home.

Wide cultivated a little patch of ground at his cottage, and Jack assisted him by carrying away the rubbish. While his master led the water on to the beds Jack worked the pump. It was a most amusing and instructive sight to see the baboon laboriously working the pump handle. He loved his master so

The Yellow Baboon.

The Yellow Baboon is an inhabitant of the West Coast regions of Africa, and has been found as far south as Mashonaland.

From Kingsley's " Natural History "

dearly that, poor fellow, he worked himself almost to death. Wide told me that sometimes he would not cease pumping until he fell exhausted. The moment he recovered his breath he went at it again as vigorously as ever.

One day a railwayman quarrelled with Wide and made offensive remarks, whereupon Jack jostled the man off the platform after the manner of a footballer at Soccer, and defied him to return. The man wisely retreated.

On another occasion a burly railway foreman in Sunday attire began playing with Jack, and started to hustle him over the edge of the platform. Jack entered into the spirit of the game, and shouldered the man so violently off the platform that he fell heavily. Rising, he seized a stick, and, with an oath, advanced threateningly on the baboon. Quick as thought Jack picked up a dirty coal-sack and belaboured his antagonist so soundly that he, too, very wisely retreated.

A gentleman told me how he watched Jack adjusting the trolley on the rails in front of his master's cottage. This job completed, he went into the cottage for Wide's walking-stick, which had been forgotten, and, on emerging, he carefully locked the door and handed both key and stick to his master, who was sitting on the trolley.

When Jack was first employed to work the levers at the signal station, passengers raised a strong protest on the score of risk of accident, but the baboon never failed during his many years of work; and on several occasions he acted in a manner simply astounding to those who have not had personal experience of the high degree of intelligence possessed by these animals.

After nine years of good and faithful service, Jack developed tuberculosis, and, after six months' illness, died on April 9, 1890. Wide was broken-hearted over the death of his one and only friend, and although he is still alive (Dec. 1918), the memory of his old companion and friend is as green as ever.

I obtained all the information possible about Jack the Signalman from a number of old Uitenhage residents, and then interviewed Mr Wide, who corrected my notes and supplied additional facts.

When telling me the story of Jack's life, from the time he purchased him when half-grown until he died nine years later, the old man was repeatedly overcome by his feelings. Tears streamed down his careworn cheeks, and he sobbed aloud in the intensity of his grief when recalling the various in-cidents of what, he declared, was the happiest time of his life, when he and Jack were chums whom nothing but cruel death could separate.

There are many who will doubtless in their superior wisdom disbelieve much of what I have related, but nevertheless the account is absolutely true, and has been set down without any embellish-ments. There are many residents in Uitenhage still living who remember Jack and his wonderful exploits.

THE CAPE BABOON OR BAVIAN

The written statements of twenty-five of these ladies and gentlemen have been filed in the Port Elizabeth Museum for future reference, should doubt be thrown on the accuracy of their story.

Like other animals, the Chacma Baboon, when hard pressed by hunger or thirst, loses its dread of man, or rather overcomes its fear of him when faced with death from starvation or thirst. I have known of several cases of native women having been driven from the mealie and Kafir corn-fields by troops of hungry baboons. A friend, when trekking with an ox-wagon, was accompanied by his wife and a Hottentot woman. He had occasion, early one morning, to go out after a herd of game, taking his two native men with him. In about half an hour's time a large troop of baboons came into view from a barren, stony ridge, and, barking furiously to keep up their courage, they advanced on the wagon. The lady and her servant walked a few paces in their direction, and threw some stones at them. The old leader, however, steadily advanced, followed by his hesitating troop. The women grew alarmed, and, retreating to the wagon, entered the tent with which it was provided, and laced up the ends. Seeing them retreat in alarm, the baboons now lost all sense of fear, and came down with a run. Surrounding the wagon, they overturned everything in their eagerness to find food. Discovering half a sack of mealie meal, they squabbled and fought over it, each doing his utmost to fill his cheek-pouches with the meal.

Finding nothing else of an edible nature, they disappeared amongst the rocks.

In Rhodesia, during a spell of dry weather, the baboons in the Matoppo Mountains were hard pressed for food ; so much so that one morning at about eight o'clock, when everybody was at breakfast, a large troop of them made a sudden dash for the mule stables at the Terminus Hotel, and succeeded in stuffing their cheek-pouches full of mealies from the bins before the alarm was raised. Then each seized a handful of the mealies and made off to their rocky home, evidently well satisfied at having outwitted their enemies—the human folk.

Baboons and monkeys are often caught in a rather novel way. Gourds are prepared with a hole at the end just large enough for the animal to thrust in its open hand. Mealies are put into the gourd, and the ape takes a fistful and hasn't the sense to drop them when it finds it cannot withdraw its clenched hand. Steel netting is sometimes used instead of gourds. I have also seen an iron-barred frame used for the same purpose.

A sub-species or local race of the Chacma Baboon occurs in the Transvaal. It is known as *Papio porcarius griseipes.*

A full account of the life and habits of the baboons of South Africa, and considerable numbers of anecdotes about them, may be seen on reference to my book entitled *The Monkeyfolk of South Africa.*

THE YELLOW BABOON

(Papio cynocephalus)

THE Yellow Baboon is an inhabitant of the West Coast regions of Africa, and is found as far south as Mashonaland.

Its habits are, in practically every way, similar to those of the Cape or Chacma Baboon. It has the reputation of being bolder and less afraid of man than the Chacma. This is not in any way due to its possessing a more resolute or fearless nature, but simply because it has learned that the natives with whom it comes in contact are not foes to be feared overmuch. In South Africa, in the wilder districts where the Chacma Baboons have not come into conflict with the European with his firearm, they too are often inclined to be aggressive, and instances have been related to me of Kafir herd-boys having been threatened and compelled to retreat and summon help.

The Yellow Baboon is so called because of the yellowish hue of its fur. It is somewhat slighter in build than the Chacma.

The two species can be recognised by the following differences :

CHACMA BABOON—Skin of the face dull ashy black; hair on the upper parts brown, and ringed indistinctly.

YELLOW BABOON—Skin of the face flesh-coloured. The hair of the upper parts ringed yellow and black.

THE GALAGO

THE galagos are lemur-like, arboreal animals. They are confined to Africa, and inhabit the forest regions from Natal to the Soudan.

Although there are only two well-known and typical species of galagos in South Africa, yet six species have been, so far, recorded as occurring south of the Zambesi.

GARNETT'S GALAGO
(Galago garnetti)

Garnett's Galago, which is better known to colonists as the Night Ape (*Nacht Aapje*), and also as the Bush Baby, is an inhabitant of the wooded districts of Natal, Zululand, and Eastern Africa generally.

It is strictly arboreal and nocturnal. It is a meek-looking little animal, and is quiet and gentle in its ways, and lives in the trees, frequenting the secluded bush-country, being generally found in the thickest part of the bush in the quietest and gloomiest portions of the forest. During the daytime it sleeps peacefully coiled up in the fork of a tree, usually near the top. Viewed in this position from below it is

Garnett's Galago.

(*a*) Garnett's Galago (*Galago garnetti*). This is the typical Galago of Natal, where it is generally known as the Bush Baby. General colour dull grey with a tinge of yellow. Hair soft and thick.

From a mounted specimen in the Port Elizabeth Museum.

(*b*) Garnett's Galago on the ground. Galagos are awkward and slow on the ground, but are marvellously agile and graceful when aloft among the branches of a tree. Garnett's Galago measures fourteen inches from the tip

hardly distinguishable from a bird's nest. Cavities in the large branches or trunks of old forest trees are favourite lurking-places of this galago, and so, too, are the abandoned nests of the larger bush-frequenting birds.

Once I shot one of these pretty little galagos, and before it died it gazed at me with a world of reproach in its big, brown, gentle-looking eyes, and that look, which had in it a world of sadness, has haunted me ever since.

These galagos can travel from branch to branch and tree to tree with great rapidity, springing several feet at a bound, and their movements are exceedingly graceful and very deliberate. They rarely descend to the ground. If surprised in an isolated tree, the galago, if hard pressed, will drop to the ground and make off at a fairly fast gallop to the nearest cover, into which it will vanish. It is futile to attempt to chase a galago in its native habitat, so swiftly does it travel amongst the branches. Their feet are prehensile, and can in consequence take a firm, strong grip of twigs and branches. So accurately and swiftly can they spring, that birds often fall victims to them, for, lying concealed at sundown on a branch, a galago will launch itself at a bird on a twig, even ten feet or more distant, and securing it, will on the instant obtain a secure footing.

The diet of the galago consists of any kinds of small lizards, edible insects, fruits, the gum which oozes from the trunk and branches of the acacia tree, buds, flowers, shoots, &c. During the summer months a heavy toll is levied on bird life, for the galago is especially fond of birds' eggs and the fledglings. Taking advantage of the darkness when birds are roosting, the galago steals silently within a few feet of them, and with a spring the victim is seized with the jaws or hands, and quickly killed. The galago, however, takes good care not to interfere with the " Bush Hawk's " domestic arrangements, for both male and female hawk are well able to defend their eggs and young against the attacks of this little night prowler.

Garnett's Galago is occasionally seen in captivity. It is gentle and interesting in its ways, and is easily tamed. Its habits and ways are very similar to those of the well-known lemurs of Madagascar which are so common in Zoological Gardens. A peculiarity which distinguishes the galago from its close relations the lemurs, is its power of folding down the upper half of its big, round, leafy-looking ears, so as to cover the orifice of the aural passage, and thus prevent the entrance of moisture from the dew-laden foliage the animal rambles through in its nocturnal peregrinations. The ears being so large and thin they are liable to get torn with twigs and thorns, and for this reason alone the power of folding down the ears is a good and useful one, for the galago is practically destitute of weapons of offence and defence ; therefore its only protection against its many enemies lies in its acute sense of hearing, hence the reason for its large, leaf-like, sensitive ears. When alarmed the galago flits as silently as a bird, and almost as swiftly through the forest, leaping lightly and gracefully from branch to branch, and to astonishing distances. They, moreover, leap with the greatest precision and certainty. I have seen them spring from a branch a distance of twenty feet through the air and alight upon a twig as gracefully and confidently as a bird; and in a moment of time springing away again as great a distance. The agility and endurance of a galago is almost unbelievable, when at home high up in a forest tree. Once we surprised a galago in an isolated tree. Two of us climbed up the tree, which was a comparatively small one, hoping to fatigue the animal by forcing it to leap from one part of the tree to another; our endeavour being to keep it on the move all the time.

Although we were tough and wiry in those days, and used to climbing trees and scaling krantzes, yet both of us were completely exhausted, while the galago seemed as fresh and full of vigour as ever.

The galago is beset by many enemies. The eagle-owls are ever on the watch to make a meal of one. Sitting bunched up and immovable upon a branch, high up in a forest tree, the eagle-owl drops like a stone upon any unwary galago which might pass beneath; and once in the clutch of this great bird's cruel talons, it is doomed.

The South African Python, with body contorted to represent the innocent branch of a tree, watches in silence throughout the warm summer's night, ready to seize and swallow any of these graceful little creatures which, in their gambols from branch to branch, might approach within striking distance.

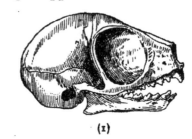

(1)

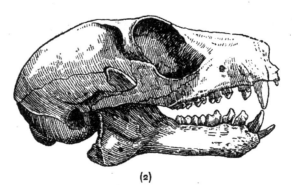

(2)

Skulls of the two typical South African Galagos.—(1) Moholi Galago (*Galago moholi*) ; (2) Garnett's Galago (*Galago garnetti*). The skulls are natural size.

Again, escaping these formidable enemies, the serval, the Kafir cat, and the leopard are ever on the watch for it. During the daytime, when it is half blind, and therefore more or less helpless, the galago is pounced upon by certain of the species of eagles which, spying it lying coiled up asleep in the fork of

74

The Moholi Galago.

The gentle little Moholi Galago sits indolently, and lazily glances around, but when alarmed he bounds off with prodigious leaps, and vanishes in the twinkling of an eye amongst the foliage of his leafy home.

a tree as they skim over the foliage, drop down upon it.

When studying bird life in Natal I was in the habit of making records of the number of eggs in a clutch, the colour, size, &c., and was, in consequence, frequently obliged to climb trees. At these times I often surprised Galagos coiled up in birds' nests, such as the abandoned nests of eagles, the larger hawks, Hammerkops (*Scopus umbretta*), &c. At other times I found them in the old nest-holes of hornbill birds, and in hollow tree trunks. It was, however, more usual to find them asleep, lying like a ball of fur amongst the dense masses of creepers on the tops of forest trees, or in the forks of the branches, usually thirty feet or more from the ground.

Garnett's Galago is dull grey with a tinge of yellow: fur close and soft, and slaty at the bases. Faint white stripe from the nose to between the eyes. Ears black and nearly destitute of hairs. Hands and feet blackish. Chin and sides yellowish white. Snout long.

Length of head and body, 14 to 15 inches. Tail to end of hairs at the tip, 11 inches.

THE MOHOLI GALAGO
(*Galago moholi*)
Ngwanangwaila of Basutos (*Kirby*)

The Moholi Galago is also popularly known as the Bush Baby, and Night Ape (*Nacht Aapje*). It is

75

smaller than Garnett's Galago; its snout is short, and its tail is more bushy towards the tip than near the base.

On the contrary, Garnett's Galago is more than twice the size of the Moholi Galago; its snout is more elongated, and its tail is of equal bushiness for its entire length.

The Moholi Galago inhabits the forest districts of the Transvaal, and extends northwards through Rhodesia to Nyasaland and neighbouring districts.

Lydekker regards this galago as a sub-species of the Senegal Galago (*Galago senegalensis*).

In Southern Rhodesia the Moholi Galago is quite common, and is frequently captured by colonists and kept in captivity. It is easily tamed, and will eat freely of practically any food substance, although meat is preferred to any other form of food.

I had one of these galagos in captivity at the Port Elizabeth Museum for a considerable time. It lay all day coiled up asleep with its bushy tail wrapped round its body, and if disturbed appeared, as a general rule, to be more or less torpid. It could not endure bright light, and always crept into the darkest corner of its cage. If placed out in the strong light it was quite bewildered. At dusk it changed its nature entirely. Instead of being sluggish, dull and listless, peering through mere slits of eyes, it was as if electrified, and its eyes were large and luminous.

One day about sundown, when placing food and water in its cage, the attendant gave it a rude poke with his finger, the top of which the galago seized and nipped, and with a yell the man jerked his hand away. This behaviour scared the animal, and with one spring it was out of the open door, then on to the top of the cage. From this point of vantage it sprang a distance of twelve feet up to the skeleton of a whale. Then we saw several brownish streaks here and there, and the galago had vanished. We searched the entire museum without success. In a corner we had on exhibition an aviary of beautiful Spanish albino doves. The following morning we found two of these dead, one of which had been partially eaten, and the other was minus its brain. Again we searched in vain, and on the next morning two doves were found to be wounded and the partially eaten body of another lay on the floor. This occurred for four or five nights. Then a tempting bait was laid down and surrounded with a mass of string, on which bird-lime had been smeared. We found the string the following morning covered with fur, but no galago. We caught the murderer at last in the very act of killing a dove. Creeping into the museum after dark, we silently waited. After a time, hearing the doves fluttering, my two friends ran from their place of concealment towards the cage, and at the same instant I switched on the electric lights. The wire mesh of the cage was just large enough for the galago to squeeze through, but we succeeded in frightening it back before it could push through and escape. It then retired to a dark corner of the cage and squatted, bunched up in as small a space as pos-

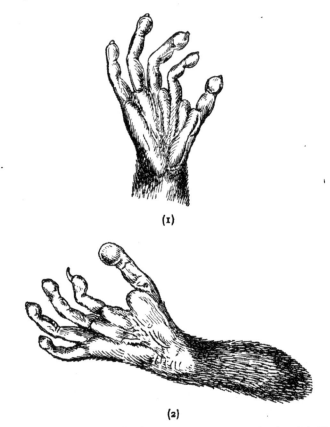

(1)

(2)

Hand and foot of a Moholi Galago (*Galago moholi*).—(1) Hand ; (2) Foot. Note the claw on the second toe. The rest of the toes, as well as the fingers of the hand, have flat nails.

sible, with its long tail tightly coiled round its body ; and so it at last was captured.

This galago, and others which I have kept in captivity, ate the dead bodies of birds in preference to fruits or a general mixed diet, indicating that in their native home a large proportion of the diet is of an animal nature, such as birds and their young.

Albinism occurs with these galagos, as with other species of animals. Two albinos were captured in a forest in Southern Rhodesia and were kept in captivity by a friend for some years.

The Moholi Galago is brownish grey on the back, gradually becoming lighter on the sides. In the males the under parts are yellowish ; in the female paler. Throat and chin white ; a white line along the nose ; eyes ringed with black ; tail rather thinly covered with brown, of the same colour its entire length, but more bushy towards the tip. Head round and nose blunt.

Length of head and body, viz. from nose to base of tail, 7 inches. Tail to end of terminal hairs, 8 inches.

THE GREAT GALAGO

(*Galago crassicaudatus*)

The Great Galago is so called because of its comparatively large size, it being as large as an average domestic cat. It is, with the exception of one closely allied species from the West Coast, the largest of the galagos. It is an inhabitant of Mossambique and the Zambesi regions, and having been found south of that river it is, in consequence, recorded as one of the South African fauna.

The Great Galago usually sleeps by day amongst the fronds of the cocoa-nut palms, and when alarmed it springs through the air from one palm to another, and it is quite useless attempting to follow it up with the idea of capturing it alive. There is only one way by which it is captured. A pot of palm wine is left on the trunk of a palm tree, and perceiving it, the galago drinks so freely of the fermented juice that it actually gets drunk, falls to the ground, and staggers about at random.

·Its diet and habits, both in its native habitat and in captivity, are practically similar to those of the other galagos.

There are three other species of galagos included amongst the South African animals. One is the Zululand Galago (*Galago zuluensis*), which has been found to occur in Zululand ; Grant's Galago (*Galago granti*), and the Mossambique Galago (*Galago mossambicus*) from the north-east corner of the forest regions of South Africa.

FLYING MAMMALS

BATS are remarkable creatures for the reason that they are the only mammal class of animals which possess wings and can fly. There are other animals, such as the Flying Squirrels and Phalangers, that have a membrane attached to the fore and hind legs, as well as the sides of the body. By stiffening the legs and holding them straight out, these animals are able to sail through the air to a limited distance, but only at an angle in a downward direction, such as from the top of a high tree to the branch of a lower one. However, this cannot be called flying. The bat, on the contrary, can fly as efficiently as a bird.

The ancestors of the bat, no doubt, developed membraneous attachments similar to those of the Flying Squirrels, and in the process of time, this arrangement became more specialised. The front leg bones increased in length, and the membrane eventually enveloped the spaces between the long fingers ; and, instead of only being able to fly in a sloping direction downwards towards the earth, from a high tree, or crag, the bat was enabled to propel itself at will through the air in all directions. On examination the wings will be seen to be composed of a thin but strong dark membrane. When flying this is spread and held out by means of what were once five toes or fingers. Four of these can easily be seen in the membrane of the wing. The fifth, or thumb, sticks out at right angles, and is only attached at one end. The tip is armed with a hook or nail, and is used by the bat to suspend its body when desiring to rest, as well as an aid in climbing. The back legs are small and serve as a back attachment for the membranes of the wings. They too have claws which are used as hands for gripping twigs, &c., when the bat is resting, and in grasping fruit which the bat desires to devour.

There are two great groups of bats. They are known as the Fruit Bats and the Insectivorous Bats. The Fruit Bats are different in appearance to those of the other group, and although there are scores of different kinds or species, yet if one only is carefully examined and compared with an Insectivorous Bat, it is sufficient to enable the student to at once distinguish Fruit Bats from those of the other kind.

Fruit Bats are large in size, their heads are dog-shaped, the wings, ears, and tail are different to the insectivorous group. The crowns of their molar teeth are smooth, or nearly so, whereas those of the insect-eating bats have points or cusps. The end of the second finger, as well as the first, is usually provided with a claw. On the contrary, Insectivorous Bats only have one claw or nail, which is on the thumb.

Epauletted Fruit Bats.

(*a*) A female Epauletted Fruit Bat in the act of flying. Note the
distended thumb on the shoulder of the left wing. When
the wings are extended to their fullest length they measure
twenty-one inches from tip to tip.

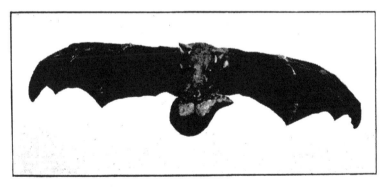

(*b*) A male Epauletted Fruit Bat in the act of flying off with a fig.

THE EPAULETTED FRUIT BAT

All species of Insectivorous Bats are small; whereas some of the Fruit Bats are very large. One of them is known as the Kalong or Malay Flying Fox (*Pteropus edulis*). It inhabits some of the islands of the Malay Archipelago, and is a giant among its kind, for it measures three feet from tip to tip of its outspread wings. It is killed and eaten for food by the Malays.

THE EPAULETTED FRUIT BAT

(Epomophorus wahlbergi)
Syn.: *E. gambianus*

THIS large bat is common on the eastern side of South Africa from the Cape Province northwards. It is very widespread, for it is found right through Africa as far north as Gambia on the west, to Kilimanjaro on the east. It is an inhabitant of the forests, wooded kloofs, and in fact wherever there are trees in abundance. This Fruit Bat cannot possibly be mistaken for one of the insectivorous kind by reason of its size, for it is a giant in comparison with any of the South African species of insect-eating bats. The bulk of its body is that of a man's closed hand, and the wings, when stretched to their fullest extent, measure on an average twenty inches from tip to tip. The male is slightly larger than the female. The Epauletted Fruit Bat is so called because of a sac or depression on each shoulder, which is marked with a patch of long white hairs. This sac or pit can be turned inside out. These two white patches on the shoulders give the animal the appearance of wearing epaulettes. They are absent or rudimentary in the female. A distinguishing feature of this bat is its large loose lips, which can be considerably distended; and the tufts of white hairs on the margins of the ears. These are present in both sexes.

The Epauletted Fruit Bats have been separated into several species. They are all confined to Africa.

There is only one young bat produced at a birth. The little creature clings tight to its mother's abdomen with its hind claws, and its mouth is usually attached to one of the teats. So close does it grip, and so snugly does it nestle, that it is invisible, except when viewed at a very short distance. When at rest the parent folds one or both of her wings over it.

This not only completely hides it from view, but keeps it dry and warm. It is suckled by the mother until sufficiently developed to be able to fly and care for itself. One which I kept in captivity gave birth to a young one, which clung close to her breast, with one or other of the teats all the time in its mouth. As it grew in size and strength, it would at times leave the mother and climb about the twigs in the cage. Eventually it ceased to cling to her, and roosted on a twig by itself. By this time it was able to fly efficiently.

The Epauletted Fruit Bat is known, or at least

A male Epauletted Fruit Bat hanging from a branch. Note
the white epaulet on the shoulder; also the white spot at
the base of the ear. (This picture is about half natural
size.)

should be, to every resident in the eastern parts of
the Cape Province, Natal, Transvaal, and Rhodesia,
for they are common in parks, gardens, and adjacent
bush-lands. All fruit-growers are well acquainted
with the Fruit Bat, for, as its name implies, its diet
consists of fruit. It is nocturnal, but is sometimes
seen flying among the trees shortly after sundown.

Ripe fruit is easy of digestion, and as it is a watery
diet, a considerable quantity is necessary to be eaten
to provide the requisite food-elements for the bodily
needs of this large bat. It knows this full well, for
its appetite is prodigious. In captivity I fed one of
these bats on bananas, and when allowed to eat to
repletion it actually ate four times its own bulk and
weight of bananas in one day. The havoc wrought
in fruit gardens by the Fruit Bat is very great. All
kinds of fruit are eaten. The Epauletted Fruit Bat
has two ways of dining. By a special adaptation of
the gullet, windpipe, and lips it is able to make an
efficient suction engine of its mouth. Finding a
nice, soft, ripe fruit, it is enveloped by the flabby,
indiarubber-like lips, which close tight around it.
The suction apparatus is then set working, and the
pulpy contents of the fruit are quickly extracted and
swallowed. The skin and pip or stone are rejected.
These bats are particularly fond of ripe figs, and
prefer them to almost any other kind of fruit. However, they levy a heavy toll upon all kinds of fruit.

A friend, thinking to outwit these destructive
bats, enveloped his ripening figs in muslin bags ; but

the crafty bats sucked the contents of the figs through the muslin.

Those fruits which do not permit of the pulp or fleshy part being extracted by means of suction, are taken in the mouth and carried to a quiet retreat, which may be within a few yards, or a mile distant. However, unless disturbed, the bat always returns to the same spot, and, hanging from a twig by one of its hind legs, with the aid of the other leg and its thumbs, the fruit is devoured, and the skin, pip or stone dropped to the ground. Sometimes the bat hangs by one of its thumbs, and uses the other one and both hind feet to hold the fruit while it is being eaten. In a short while, sometimes as much as a barrow-load of leavings accumulate. Taking advantage of this habit of flying with the stolen fruit to the same twig, I managed to capture quite a number of these bats by spreading linen thread with birdlime and hanging it close to the twig. This limed thread clung tenaciously to the creature's soft fur, and entangled the wings so thoroughly that the bat fell to the ground helpless.

When squabbling with each other in a fruit tree over the choicest fruit, they utter discordant squeaks. It is wonderful to observe how rapidly one of these bats can settle on a twig. Many a time I have sat hidden under a large fruit tree on bright moonlight nights and watched the fruit bats alighting on twigs, and devouring the fruit or carrying it off to some retreat. Flying into the tree, the bat seizes a twig

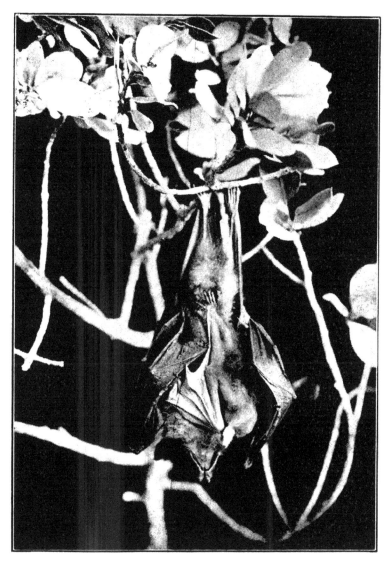

An Epauletted Fruit Bat and its baby clinging to its breast.
When the air grew cold the mother carefully folded her wing
over the little one to keep it warm.

with one or both hind legs, and on the same instant the wings close tight. If a fruit is not within reach, it climbs along to it. Often the bat hovers over the desired morsel with expanded wings and seizes it in its mouth or takes bites out of it without alighting.

When shot at or otherwise molested, Fruit Bats become very suspicious and cunning, and take to visiting the orchards late in the night or towards morning.

In Natal they robbed my orchard to such an extent that I declared war against them ; but after shooting half a dozen I found it necessary to sit up late into the night, and even then only succeeded in killing one or two. Their sight and hearing are keen and sharp, and after being frightened once or twice by being shot at, they are so wary that unless you carefully conceal yourself you will fail to get a shot at them.

Fruit Bats are without any redeeming qualities, so far as man is concerned, for they rob him in a wholesale way of his fruit. They not only eat a great quantity, but they are exceedingly wasteful. For several mornings I examined their refuse heaps and found that some fruits had barely been tasted—they were evidently not to the liking of the thief and were dropped. Others were partly eaten, and on the skins and pips of most of them a portion of the edible pulp remained. Then again, in squabbling with each other over the fruit, and in their attempts to take it in their mouths, quantities are detached from the twigs and drop to the ground.

When there are no orchards to rob, these bats betake themselves to the forest trees and feast upon the buds, flowers, berries, and wild fruits. In the past they have acted as efficient agents in sewing the seeds of native trees and shrubs far and wide, for the fertility of the seeds which are swallowed is not impaired in the least by passing through their bodies.

All species of Fruit Bats may safely be classed as foes to the human race. On the approach of dawn the Fruit Bat flies off to some safe retreat in the shadiest part of a forest, and roosts among the branches. When sleeping, it grips a twig with one or both hind claws, and hangs suspended with its wings folded. When the weather is wet or cold, the head is enveloped by a portion of one wing. On the slightest alarm the bat drops from its perch and flies off through the foliage, and is instantly lost sight of. They often congregate in great numbers at the roosting-places, chattering, squeaking, and quarrelling over the possession of the most favourable spots in which to pass the night.

The most favoured sleeping-places about towns and villages are the old gum trees, under the loose bark of which they sleep, or on which they hang. Several of them were hanging to the rough bark of a gum tree within a dozen feet of me, yet although I was looking direct at them, they were barely discer-

nible owing to the dull mouse colour of their fur
and dark wings blending so perfectly with the colour
of the bark of the tree.

It by no means follows, if Fruit Bats are in the
habit of visiting an orchard at night, that they are
roosting in the vicinity during the daytime. They
may be resting in the orchard itself, or their sleeping-
place may be many miles away in some lonely kloof.
When food is scarce, Fruit Bats range over great
distances. Sometimes there happens to be a farm
away out upon the veld, five to ten miles from any
trees suitable for roosting-places for these bats, and
the farmer is puzzled to account for their presence in
his orchard at night, as he can find no trace of them
during the day. Possibly the bats had flown from
some distant spot five to ten miles away, returning
before dawn. I have at intervals for a number of
years kept Epauletted Fruit Bats in captivity in large
aviaries where they had plenty of room to fly. It is
an interesting sight to see them climbing about the
twigs in the cage, using their thumbs as we would our
fingers. On the ground they are very awkward and
crawl about in a most ungainly manner. When hanging suspended by both hind feet, if a fruit was handed
to one of them, it detached one foot from the twig,
and with a rapid stroke drove the claws into it.
Then, grasping the twig with the thumb of one or
both wings, it freed the other foot, the claws of which
were also driven into the fruit. Thus secured it
was leisurely devoured.

When the food was placed in a dish upon the ground, a great scramble ensued ; some of the bats flew down, others hastily climbed down the branches in the cage, hand over hand. Then they all began to squabble, striking out at each other with their claw-armed thumbs, and threatening one another with gaping jaws. In the public parks and gardens of Port Elizabeth and Walmer, these bats may be seen and heard nightly. When calling to each other the note is very high pitched, and sounds very much like the metallic ringing noise produced by sharply striking a blacksmith's anvil with a metal hammer. They are, in consequence, called Anvil Bats. For many years past in Natal and the Cape Provinces a newspaper controversy has, at intervals, been waged as to the origin of this shrill noise, so commonly heard at night, the majority of people claiming that it was the call of a bird. On one occasion I was bold enough to write to the press and deny this assertion, and mentioned that it was a Fruit Bat which was the originator. I was instantly assailed by a score of correspondents who wrote to the newspaper declaring in the most positive terms that it was a bird— the Anvil Bird. Many had seen it, and actually described its appearance, which, in most cases, tallied with the bird known as the Night Jar. Once an erroneous popular belief gets established it is hard to overthrow. For many years I have made it my business with pen and tongue to attack erroneous popular beliefs, and have brought down consider-

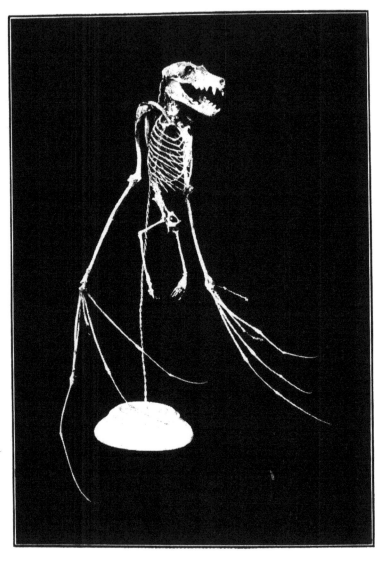

The skeleton of an Epauletted Fruit Bat. (Note the enormously elongated arms and fingers.)

able opprobrium upon myself in consequence. The less a man knows of any subject, the more positive are his assertions, as a general rule, in regard to it.

The Epauletted Fruit Bat has a tail, but it is very small, and is invisible unless searched for in the thick fur between the hind legs. However, there are some species of Epauletted Fruit Bats which are tailless.

During the months of December and January I have often secured female Fruit Bats with half-grown young ones clinging to their breasts.

Although common from the Cape to the Sahara, the Epauletted Fruit Bat is unknown in Madagascar. This is rather surprising, as it is not very far from the mainland of East Africa.

The Epauletted Fruit Bats in South Africa have been separated into three species—the two others are as follows : *Epomophorus crypturus ; Epomophorus angolensis.*

THE COLLARED FLYING FOX

(Rousettus leachi)
Syn.: *R. collaris*

The Collared Flying Fox is another Fruit Bat of large size, which, at a distance, is similar in appearance to the Epauletted Fruit Bat. On close inspection, however, it is seen to differ a great deal. The

Epauletted Fruit Bats have large, flabby, distensible lips ; there are tufts of white hair at the basis of the ears, and in the case of the males there is the characteristic white shoulder patch. The Collared Flying Fox, on the contrary, has no trace of white hair on it, and its lips are not large or flabby. Its fur is brown, which is darker above than on the underparts. The hair on the neck is longer and coarser than that on the body, and presents the appearance of a collar, and in the mature male it is of a deep yellow colour. The presence of this collar has given rise to the name of the bat.

The Collared Flying Fox is found in all parts of Africa from the Cape Province to the Mediterranean Ocean.

As a destroyer of fruit it is as great a pest in South Africa as its cousin the Epauletted Fruit Bat. In my fruit garden in Natal this species of bat caused great damage. It was particularly fond of loquats. Sometimes one or more of these bats would settle in a tree, and finding a bunch of loquats, selected the ripe ones and devoured them on the spot. At other times a loquat would be taken in the mouth and carried to one of the shadiest trees in the quietest part of the orchard, and here, hanging upside down from a twig, it leisurely ate the fruit, dropping the pips and skin to the ground. Journeying back and forth a single bat will, during the course of a night, make twoscore or more journeys.

Sitting concealed under a loquat tree, I kept some

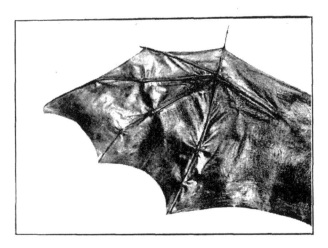

Wings of Bats.

(*a*) The wing of a Fruit Bat, showing the fingers connected
by the membrane of the wing. The thumb, which is erect,
is provided with a claw, and is used in climbing and grasping
twigs. The index finger, next to the thumb, is also provided
with a claw, which is always absent in Insectivorous Bats.

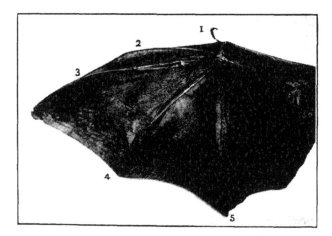

(*b*) Insectivorous Bats possess a thumb with a claw on the end
of it, as seen in this illustration. The index or forefinger,
however, in these bats is *not* tipped with a claw. On the
contrary, the South African fruit-eating bats all possess the
thumb, and a forefinger *terminated by a claw*.

(1) Thumb ; (2) index or forefinger ; (3) second finger ; (4) third
finger ; (5) fourth finger.

THE COLLARED FLYING FOX

of these Collared Flying Foxes under careful observation. Swooping down from aloft, a bat would drop
noisily into the tree. Then another and another,
until perhaps half a dozen had alighted. On first
settling, a twig was gripped with one or both hind
feet and, aided by the thumbs on the shoulders of the
wings, the bat climbed through the foliage until it
reached the coveted fruit. Sometimes several bats
approached the same bunch of loquats. When this
occurred there was much squabbling, accompanied
by discordant squeaks and chattering. On the
whole, the Collared Flying Fox is more destructive
to fruit than its cousin, for the reason that it has a
habit of hovering with quivering wings over a fruit
and taking bites out of it. In consequence it dis-
lodges great quantities, which fall to the ground, and
of course their market value is spoilt, for even if they
have not been bitten, they are more or less bruised
by falling.

This bat gives birth to one young at a birth, which
clings with its hind claws to the lower part of the
mother's body, with its face buried in the fur of the
parent's breast, and one of the teats in its mouth.
In this manner, aided by its thumbs, it clings so
tightly that it requires some little effort to pull it
away from the parent's body.

There is another species of fruit bat in South
Africa known as the Yellow Fruit Bat (*Eidolon
helvum*). It differs but little from the Collared Fruit
Bat. It is slightly larger, and its fur has a yellowish

tinge, especially in the neck region. It occurs plentifully from the vicinity of the Zambesi, northwards through Africa. I have obtained specimens from the midlands of the Cape Province, in the district of Steynsburg. All species or kinds of Fruit Bats, otherwise known as Flying Foxes, are a pest to man, and are of no economic value to him as far as is at present known.

The Insectivorous Bats

Bats are flying mammals. A mammal is a warm-blooded animal which suckles its young. Bats are all grouped in a class or order known as Chiroptera, or hand-winged, derived from the Greek word *chier*, which means "hand," and *pteron*, "wing." The bat class is divided into two sections, or sub-orders. The group called Fruit Bats are known collectively as the Megachiroptera, which means "large bats," for all the species or kinds of fruit bats are large. Those which are known as Insectivorous Bats are of smaller size than the Fruit Bat group, and are in consequence known as the Microchiroptera, which means " little bats." The Insectivorous Bats are cosmopolitan, that is, they inhabit all parts of the world. They are, however, most abundant in the tropical regions. There are hundreds of species or kinds. In South Africa alone there have been nearly half a hundred species and sub-species so far identified.

Insectivorous Bats can usually be distinguished

A Collared Flying Fox with its baby clinging to its breast.

From " Fauna of S. Africa," by W. L. Sclater.

from the Fruit Bats by their short, flattened, wizened-looking faces and small eyes. A glance at the teeth will at once settle the question, for the molars or back teeth have sharp cusps or points on their crowns or grinding surfaces. In the molars of the upper jaw the points or cusps look like the letter W. On the contrary, the cusps or crowns of the molar teeth of Fruit Bats are smooth. On examining the wing it will be found that the Insectivorous Bat has a thumb, with a claw or nail on the end of it; but the index finger, which is the one next to the thumb, has no claw at the end, as is usually the case with the Fruit Bats. If this index finger in the wing membrane has a claw at its termination, then you may be quite sure the specimen is a Fruit Bat.

The Insectivorous Bats of all species in South Africa are of the greatest possible service to man. Of his many species of animal friends these bats rank with the most useful, for the services they render the human race are considerable. Their diet consists entirely of winged insects, which issue forth in vast numbers during the early evening and night, and fly into the air in quest of their mates. Simultaneously with the insects taking wing, their foes, the Insectivorous Bats, sally forth from their shelters in caves, crannies, under the loose bark of trees, or the lofts of houses, and for hours are busy capturing and devouring insects on the wing. If an insectivorous bird which devours caterpillars is considered a valuable ally of man, then the insect-eating bats may be

95

regarded as being a hundred per cent. more useful in an economic sense, for the reason that the insects they devour are adults, every female of which is capable of producing hundreds and thousands of eggs which hatch out into caterpillars or some other form of larvæ. Therefore, every female winged insect devoured by a bat is equal to as many caterpillars and other larvæ which a pair of birds would take several days to collect. Again, many of these insects take wing prior to boring holes into trees in which to deposit eggs that will hatch out into grubs. Secure from the attacks of birds, these grubs tunnel holes through the wood and ruin it. Or it may be fruit is punctured and eggs laid inside. In due time the eggs hatch and the grub works its will on the fruit, away from the keen eyes of its enemies, the caterpillar-eating birds.

A glance at the teeth of a Fruit Bat will make it clear that its smooth-crowned molars are specially adapted for chewing up soft substances, such as fruit. On the contrary, the sharp-pointed molar teeth of the Insectivorous Bats are admirably adapted for piercing and tearing the hard horny cases of beetles and many other kinds of winged insects.

During the daytime the swallows and other insect-eating birds wage warfare upon insect pests, and the moment they retire to rest, the bats take their place. In this way the Creator has so accurately established the balance of Nature, that insects under normal conditions do not become a plague. However,

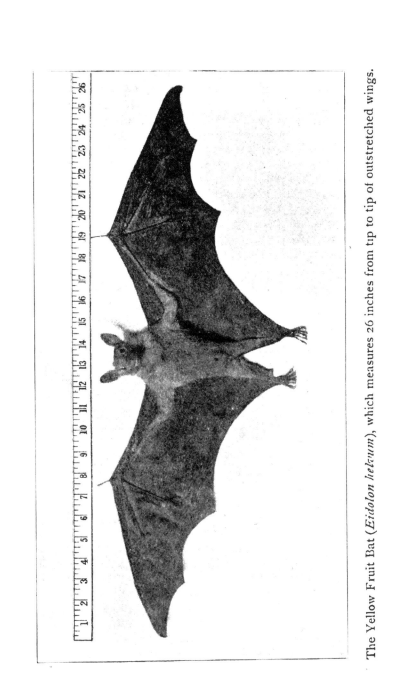

The Yellow Fruit Bat (*Eidolon helvum*), which measures 26 inches from tip to tip of outstretched wings.

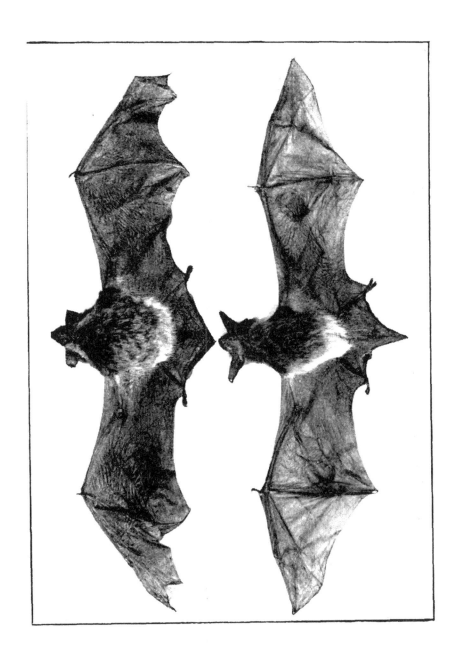

wherever man appears he foolishly interferes with
the balance of Nature by giving undue licence to his
cruelty-loving, destructive instincts.

In every South African town and village our little
friends the bats may be observed during the evening
in the summer-time busily employed in capturing
insects, including the troublesome, and in many
instances malaria-carrying, mosquito. To kill an
Insectivorous Bat is not only a cruel, wanton act—
it is a positive crime. Yet it is a common pastime
for boys, and even grown men, to amuse themselves
by shooting and otherwise killing these eminently
useful little creatures. If a bat should accidentally
fly through an open door or window into a room, an
instant rush is made by the inmates for weapons
with which to maim and kill the terrified little
creature. If there is no man-made penalty attached
to taking the lives of God's living creatures, which
have been created for a definite and useful purpose,
numbers of otherwise moral and respectable people
seem to imagine that they are at liberty to give the
fullest rein to their destructive instincts, inherited
from remote and savage ancestry, and which ere this
should have been either bred out, or converted to
some better and higher purpose than the wilful
murder of our animal friends.

In the Insectivorous Bat, the sense of touch is
marvellously developed. So sensitive are these nerve-
endings that it is not actually necessary for bats to
come into contact with any object unless they desire

to do so. In some mysterious way, probably by vibrations set up in the atmosphere, they are aware of the proximity of objects. This was proven many years ago by what would seem a rather cruel experiment, but which was undertaken in the interests of science. Bats were deprived of their sight and then allowed to fly in a room, across which silk threads were stretched at a distance apart—just sufficient to enable the bats to pass through with outstretched wings. The bats not only successfully avoided striking the ceiling or walls, but not in a single instance did they come in contact with the threads. More threads were then stretched across the room, so close together that the bats, to avoid touching them, were obliged to considerably contract their wings. This they accomplished satisfactorily. Branches were then placed in their way, and they flew in and out between the twigs and leaves, and even suspended themselves by their legs, just as efficiently as if they possessed sight.

In most of the bats this acute sense is situated in the wing membranes, and in the delicate and often large ears. However, many species of bats have curious expansions of skin on the face, usually called the " Nose leaf." In some this facial membrane is small, but in others it is both large and complicated. These nose leaves are always fringed round with delicate hairs, attached to the roots of which are exceedingly sensitive nerves.

The Fruit Bats do not possess this facial mem-

THE INSECTIVOROUS BATS

brane, but in their case the eyes are large and specially adapted for seeing clearly at night.

, Many kinds of insect-eating bats have no nose leaves, and in consequence their senses of touch are not so acute as the other kinds possessing well-developed nose membranes. The reason is that those species which do not possess nose leaves issue forth mostly during the early evening and at dawn, in search of their prey, except of course on bright moonlight nights, or in towns where there are street lights. Around these lights swarms of insects hover, which fall easy victims to the active little bats. The bats with large ears and nose leaves issue forth usually after twilight has merged into darkness, for it seems to make no difference to them whether it is pitch dark or moonlight. Their eyes are, in most instances, very tiny, and actual sight apparently does not help them much, if at all, in their movements, or capturing the flying insects on which they feed. To us who are so dependent on our eyesight, it seems hard to believe that other senses can be developed to such a degree of perfection that by means of them, and unaided by eyesight, an animal is guided to its prey, and can find its way about as well, if not better, than we can by means of sight. We are aware, for instance, there are sightless salamanders and fishes inhabiting the waters in deep caves where no ray of light ever penetrates; and we have also learned that bats seem in no way handicapped in their flight, or in selecting and suspending themselves from a perch, when deprived of their eyes.

Whether all the species of Insectivorous Bats inhabiting South Africa hibernate in the country or not is unknown. It is certain, however, that considerable numbers of them do so, for on occasional warm winter evenings they may be seen on the wing. Bats have on many occasions been brought to me which have been found in old outhouses, and up under the roof in a loft of a dwelling. These specimens were cold, and incapable of crawling or flying. When warmed they regained their summer vigour and energy, and when handled, attempted to bite, and on being thrown into the air flew away.

In Natal I have on several occasions found large clusters of bats in caves and other sheltered, dark recesses. They were all hanging suspended by the hind claws. Some of them on sight of the light flew away, but the majority remained hanging. During a winter season recently in Port Elizabeth, a north-west wind blew, which caused a sudden rise in the temperature of the air. That evening I observed several insect-eating bats hovering around the street arc-lights; and between the ceiling and the roof of a stoep under which I was sitting, I heard the shuffling and squeaking of bats, and saw two or three issue out and take wing.

The Fruit Bats in South Africa, on the contrary, do not hibernate during the winter months. Throughout the neighbourhood of Port Elizabeth

A Serotine Bat (*Vespertilio capensis*) with its baby clinging to its
body. These are the little bats which are so common all over
South Africa, and which issue forth and hawk insects on the
wing at dusk, about our houses and gardens.

The Cape Slit-faced Bat, so called because of a deep slit between
the eyes. It is common all over South Africa, and roosts by
day in lofts, the hollows of decayed trees, and in caves. It
sallies forth at night to devour noxious winged insects.

and Walmer, their shrill metallic-sounding cry may be heard, and their weird forms may be observed flitting about the trees in gardens and parks during the entire winter season.

Insectivorous Bats sometimes congregate in great numbers under the eaves of houses, between the ceiling and the roof, and other parts which it is difficult to reach without first removing a portion of the woodwork. These bats sometimes become a nuisance by reason of their shrill chattering, squeaking, and the excreta which accumulates. When this is the case, every possible means should be taken to dislodge them before resorting to taking their lives. This can frequently be done by driving them forth and blocking up or putting netting over the apertures through which they enter. They often become very troublesome in churches which are built in the old-fashioned manner, affording abundant nooks and crevices for bats to rest and hide in security. It is rather disconcerting to a preacher when a couple of bats elect to fly about a few feet above the heads of the audience during the service, ever and anon skimming within an inch of the good folks' heads and faces. Within ten miles of Pietermaritzburg in Natal, on the farm of Mr. H. Martens, a tunnel was driven into the side of a hill for a considerable distance. About fifty yards from the entrance, the tunnel takes a sharp turn, and after proceeding some yards the place is in a state of absolute darkness, where even an owl's eyes would be of no service at

all. This tunnel was made by a gold-mining syndi-
cate. With a friend I explored it, lighting our way
along with candles. When half way along the passage, which was some six feet or so broad, and as
many in height, our voices echoed and re-echoed in
the weirdest manner. Presently I heard a distant
rumbling, like the noise of the waves afar off, beat-
ing against a rocky coast. It grew louder and more
defined. Then in an instant our candles were extinguished, and a great rush as of wind swept past
us. Then the rustling of hundreds and thousands
of wings on all sides of us was heard. I instinctively covered my face with my hat, fearing that in
their wild flight through that narrow passage, in
profound darkness, some of the bats would dash in
my face. However, the precaution was needless, for
not a single bat touched either of us, although, according to a third friend, who had declined to enter
the hole, a couple of thousand bats, at least, flew out
at the entrance. Lighting our candles we again
advanced, and at every step two or three bats flitted
past within an inch or two of our faces. Eventually
we reached the end, and here, hanging from
the rough dynamite - blasted rocky sides and
roof of the tunnel, were at least a hundred bats.
On approaching within a few feet they squeaked
with terror, their bodies quivered, and the nose
leaves and ears vibrated rapidly; but until we attempted to handle them, they did not try to escape.
These bats were of at least four species—viz. the

A Cape Slit-faced Bat asleep. It is clinging to a twig with the
claws of its feet. Its large ears are exceedingly sensitive, and
are as good as eyes. Most Insectivorous Bats have tiny eyes.
If deprived of their sight, the loss does not seem to make much
difference to them.

THE INSECTIVOROUS BATS

Brown Wrinkled-lipped Bat, Cape Slit-faced Bat, Cape Horseshoe Bat, and European Horseshoe Bat.

Insectivorous Bats in South Africa usually have one young at a birth. It clings tight to the parent's bosom, with its hind feet and the clawed thumbs on its wings. It usually has one of the mother's teats in its mouth. By this means it is enabled to cling tighter. The young one holds close and firmly to the mother, and never leaves her for an instant until almost full-grown. The commonest of the insect-eating bats in South Africa are the Cape Horseshoe Bat, Cape Slit-faced Bat, several species of Serotine Bats, Bourbon Bat, Long-winged Bat, and Wrinkled-lipped Bat.

All species of Insectivorous Bats can, without question, be claimed to be of the greatest economic value to man in his hard struggle against the armies of noxious insects with which he is surrounded, and which carry disease and death to him and his flocks and herds in some instances; and in others, ruin, dire and complete, to the produce of his fields.

THE LION

(*Felis leo*)

Ingonyama, Imbubesi or Imbubi of Swazis and Zulus (*Kirby*) ; Ingonyama of Amaxosa (*Stanford*) ; Tau of Bechuanas and Basutos (*Bryden* and *Kirby*).

THE Lion is regarded as the king of wild beasts, and like Robinson Crusoe, he was " monarch of all he surveyed," until man invaded his haunts and made war upon him with his terrible weapons of destruction. The lion now experiences the novelty of being hunted himself. However, in the wilder parts of Central Africa, where civilised man rarely penetrates with his firearms, the lion still holds sway, and fearlessly roams through his domains, dining off the tenderest and most appetising parts of herbivorous animals whenever the pangs of hunger trouble him. His diet consists mainly of members of the antelope tribe. He lies in ambush and suddenly pounces out upon his prey, or, if he fails after the first rush, he makes a succession of terrific springs and leaping bounds for a hundred yards or so, travelling almost as fast as the fleetest horse ; but he cannot keep up this pace, and if not successful in his charge he gives up the chase.

Favourite resorts of lions are the water holes and other drinking places where the various animals converge in the early hours of the morning to slake their thirst. In this way they are enabled to ambush their prey. When overtaken by disease, old age, worn-out or broken fangs, the lion is no longer able to capture the alert and fleet-footed antelopes, and resorts to meaner fare, even satisfying his hunger upon rats, mice, and lizards. But he is not satisfied for long with this meagre fare, and at last screws up his courage to tackle a native; and then it dawns upon him that these black, half-naked humanfolk are very easy to kill and afford an abundance of good meat obtainable with very little effort. This destruction of human life continues until, in self-defence, the terrified villagers turn out in a strong body and put an end to the man-eater—usually after a sanguinary combat. In many parts of Africa where the villagers' goats and other domestic animals begin to mysteriously disappear, they say: " Ah, there is an old toothless lion about. We must turn out and kill him, or he will soon begin eating us."

Unless sorely pressed by hunger, a lion, fit and capable, seldom takes to killing human beings, as he has a wholesome dread of this formidable biped, and particularly so after he has once come in contact with an armed and mounted hunter. The lion is by no means the noble, courageous, fearless animal many authors, poets, and bards make him out to be. He fiercely attacks and slays other animals weaker than himself, or who possess weapons of offence or defence of a very inferior order to his.

Unless badgered, cornered, wounded, or incautiously followed into his lair, he will never attack a man unless, as previously stated, he is pressed and beset by hunger, and then he will craftily watch his opportunity to pounce upon those whom he thinks are the most defenceless. The hunter, trader, and traveller in the wilder parts of the " Dark Continent " are dreadfully pestered by the lion's fondness for bullock, horse, and donkey meat. Gordon Cumming tells a harrowing tale of a hungry lion that prowled around his camp one night, roaring in marrow-freezing manner, intent upon getting at his oxen. One of his Hottentot drivers got up from the fireside to incite the dogs to rush out and scare the " King of the Forest," and to cast a few firebrands in his direction, as lions usually have a great dread of fire. The Hottentot, immediately upon lying down again by the fireside, was pounced upon by a huge shaggy-maned lion which rushed out from the inky darkness, seized him by the back of the neck, and in spite of being belaboured by the victim's comrade with a firebrand, the lion carried his quarry away into the bush. For some hours Cumming and his men sat listening to the cracking and crunching of the Hottentot's bones, accompanied by the lion's occasional growls of satisfaction. The night being

Lions.

From Longmans' "Wild Animals of the Empire."

Photo: W. S. Berridge.

Lion Cubs.

as black as ink, and the bush on all sides thick and almost impenetrable, with many other hungry lions awaiting a chance for a meal, they were powerless to render aid, beyond firing random shots into the darkness. At early dawn they ventured out, and all they found of the Hottentot was some ragged pieces of clothing, a few mangled remains of flesh, and a boot with a foot in it.

In Rhodesia lions still give a great deal of trouble to the settlers by carrying off cattle, goats, and sheep, even venturing close to Bulawayo itself. Two were shot recently in Zululand, there still being a good many in that country, particularly in the game preserves. The numbers are doubtless much exaggerated, owing probably to the lions' habit of turning up at the most unexpected places; consequently the same troop is frequently seen in various parts of the country. One day a Government surveyor was riding his bicycle down a slope when, to his utter dismay, he saw a troop of lions gambolling about in the roadway just ahead. He promptly ran his cycle off the track as the most expeditious manner of dismounting, and got a severe tumble in consequence. Meanwhile the lions calmly watched him, he momentarily expecting to be entombed in those huge bodies, but to his intense relief they leisurely made off and away across the rugged hillside.

On another occasion a gentleman came across a troop of lions in Zululand feasting upon a zebra. He thought discretion the better part of valour and quietly retreated. A friend, who is a Government official in Zululand, was out quail-shooting when, suddenly, out of some long grass a lion sprang up, and stood for some moments glaring and growling at the terrified quail-shooter, whose past ill-deeds were doubtless flashing with lightning rapidity through his mind, as is popularly supposed to be the case when a man is in deadly peril and momentarily expecting death. What is more likely, he was too paralysed with fear to have any thoughts at all. However, the lion made off at a lumbering gallop, and thus gave the poor fellow a chance to reform his ways.

One of the Zululand magistrates some years ago captured two lion cubs. The mother, instead of boldly defending her young ones, made off into the bush. These cubs, when half-grown, were as tame as domestic kittens. They were eventually sent to the Pretoria Zoo in charge of the young man who had been in the habit of looking after them. Whenever he outspanned he used to give them their liberty. On one of these occasions his companion shot a bushbuck and deposited it at the other wagon, a quarter of a mile from where the lions were. The breeze presently changed, the lion cubs scented game, and immediately crouched with their noses elevated, and carefully crept in the direction of the buck. When within a short distance they made a terrific rush and sprang upon the body. With considerable difficulty their caretaker persuaded them to relinquish their prize. Shortly afterwards they were romping about like two kittens, when a wagon trekked past and disappeared over the brow of the slope. Presently they ceased their play and made off full speed after it. Their caretaker hastened after them, and lo and behold! they were meekly trotting behind the wagon like a pair of dogs, evidently having mistaken it for that of their owner.

In the early days of South Africa the lions had a luxurious, easy-going life of it, for game was then plentiful. The springbucks covered the plains in their hundreds of thousands, and when on the approach of the dry season they were migrating northwards to seek more favourable pasture grounds, the lions would leisurely trot along like camp followers in the rear, and dine off venison whenever they had a mind to. In those days the lion fulfilled his mission in life in keeping down the too rapid increase of herbivorous animals, which otherwise would have denuded the country of its vegetation. But on the advent of man with his firearms, the lion was no longer needed, and his extinction began, and is still proceeding.

The pagan Romans employed considerable numbers of lions at their entertainments in the Coliseum, and many thousands of Christians and prisoners of war were torn to pieces and devoured, " butchered to make a Roman holiday." Records show that over 50,000 lions were captured and brought to Rome within a period of forty years. Away back in ancient Biblical times, dens of lions were kept as executioners of criminals, the poor wretches being pitched headlong into the den, as one would fling in a lump of meat. The strength of a full-grown lion in his prime is prodigious; he can fell an ox with a blow of his paw, crunch up the bones of its neck in a moment, and drag off the whole carcase to his lair. An instance is on record of a bugler being seized by the waistband and carried off by a lion, but, after the first paralysing shock of fright, the man bethought himself of his bugle, and managed to blow a shrill blast, upon which the lion spat him out, bounded high into the air, and disappeared in the forest.

The same species of lion is found from the Cape to the Mediterranean coast and eastwards, but the different conditions of life, including climate, geographical features, &c., of the various parts of Africa and Asia have produced six varieties, which all differ considerably in coloration, scantiness or profusion of mane, &c. They are popularly known as :

(1) The Lion of Barbary. (2) The Lion of Senegal. (3) The Lion of the Cape. (4) The Bengal Lion. (5) The Persian Lion. (6) The Lion of Guzerat.

Even in South Africa there is much variation in colour, length of mane, &c. Selous has shot many black lions, and on one occasion shot a female of the ordinary tawny hue which contained two cubs, one black-haired, the other the usual colour.

The weight of a large well-developed lion averages

about 500 lbs. The lion makes his den by scratching away the earth in sóme very retired and secluded locality, and if not disturbed will remain there and issue forth during the hours of darkness, intent upon slaying some unfortunate beast. When he has depleted the neighbourhood of game, he betakes himself to some other hunting-ground. He hunts entirely by night, and sleeps off his feast during the day, and if disturbed or attacked in the daytime he seems ill at ease, and not nearly so bold as at night. There is a quotation about " those whose deeds are evil, love darkness," which aptly applies to this flesh-eating beast, and it seems the darker the night the bolder he becomes, and particularly so on dark, wild, stormy nights. It is on those nights the hunter sits under or in his wagon listening to the terrific roaring of the lions prowling round his camp, intent upon devouring his cattle, and leaving him·and his wagon stranded in the wilderness. Dr. Livingstone mentions the fact that the lion frequently, as a change of diet, feeds upon the desert water-melon (*Cuicumis caffer*), which the desert lands of Africa, after an unusual downfall of rain, are literally covered with, affording both food and drink to hosts of different species of herbivorous animals. In the Kalahari water is very scarce and frequently unobtainable, and these juicy melons, no doubt, are at times eaten by lions to slake their thirst. There is no doubt about the fact that the lion frequently devours the paunch of its victim, with its contents of half-digested grass and other herbage, and in this way he gets the benefit of a cooling alkaline diet to counteract the acid re-action of a flesh diet.

On the approach of the breeding season there are many frightful combats among the lions. When the battles are finally over the lion and his mate live affectionately together until the young have grown sufficiently to take care of themselves. The lion at this time is very unselfish, for he invariably brings his " kill " to his mate, and allows her to help herself first. So long as the cubs are small he carefully guards them and their mother.

The period of gestation of the lioness is about 108 days, and she produces two to five at a birth—generally three. When the cubs are a few months old they begin to practise the art of stalking, hunting, and slaying, and at the age of about three years their education is complete, and they then usually wander away from their parents.

The opinions expressed by various hunters in regard to the lion's roar are very contradictory, some claiming that it is no more awe-inspiring or impressive than the booming cry of the cock ostrich, but this is without doubt a libel. The lion's roar is deep-toned, and repeated in rapid succession, louder and louder, then the volume of sound gradu-ally dies away and fades into a muffled muttering. At other times the lion gives voice to a low, deep, moaning sound, repeated several times, ending in a loud sighing noise. Those who compare the lion's roar with the cry of the cock ostrich have evidently never been camped out in the desolate wilds on a stormy night with half a score of lions prowling around, mingling their horrifying roars with the moanings of the gathering storm and distant rumblings of thunder. The stoutest heart quails with fear under such circumstances.

Some years ago a hunter on the quest for lions in Northern Rhodesia discovered the remains of the skeletons of a lion and male gemsbuck. The latter's long lance-like horns were tightly wedged through the ribs of the lion; and the neck-bones of the gemsbuck, crushed and broken, indicated that both had died in mortal combat. The lion had doubtless made his spring, and the gemsbuck spitted him on his horns. Possibly this is of more frequent occurrence than is supposed, as jackals and other carnivorous animals would naturally destroy all traces in the majority of instances.

After killing an animal the lion's first proceeding is usually to disembowel the victim and bury the entrails, in order, it is thought, to conceal the odour given off by them, for fear of attracting other carnivorous animals.

Mr. Anderson, the naturalist, relates an instance of seeing a lion and lioness fighting over the body of an antelope, which eventually resulted in the death of the lioness and the devouring of a considerable portion of her flesh by her mate.

Lions breed freely in captivity, and rear their

young, which develop into fine strong lions. Sometimes the cubs, when born, are taken away from the mother and reared by a dog whose own puppies have been destroyed, as it sometimes happens the mother refuses to rear her cubs. At the Dublin Zoological Gardens considerable numbers of lions are bred and disposed of to various zoological gardens and menageries. When I last visited that town, a lioness had four sturdy cubs three months old. Another had two a month old.

It is possible to produce what are termed lion-tiger hybrids by mating the lion and tiger. In the wild state this is unheard of, although in some parts of Asia lions and tigers are found in the same localities. Mr. Carl Hagenbeck succeeded in breeding a lion-tiger hybrid which eventually attained a size and weight equal to that of the largest lions known. Its weight was 467 lbs. Its head and tail were lion-like, but its body was more or less striped like that of a tiger, and it had no mane.

Two more were born of a lion father and a tigress mother. They both took after the tigress, being more tiger-like in shape and markings than the lion. Several others have been born, some being lion-like, others more like the tiger. These mules or hybrids, however, are quite sterile, as is the case with all mules. It is well that Nature has ordained that this shall be so, for otherwise there would soon be a mongrel race of wild animals on the face of the earth. As it is, every species remains quite distinct. If a hybrid is produced by man's ingenuity, this abnormality cannot be perpetuated.

Lions are now extinct in South Africa southward of the Orange River. They are still to be found in Zululand, the wilder parts of the Transvaal, the Kalahari, and in Rhodesia, as well as German South-west Africa. Various writers mention that lions were plentiful near Capetown as late as the year 1801. Kolben says that in 1707 they were quite common in the vicinity of the town. The last lion recorded from the Cape Colony was one killed near Commetjes Post in 1842. In Natal the last one recorded was shot by General Bisset in 1865.

In 1897 a lion was killed at Springs near Johannesburg, and another the following year at Heidelburg, south of Johannesburg. At present the lion ranges from the northern parts of South Africa right through Africa and Southern Asia as far as North-west India. In Great Britain and Europe the lion was formerly common, as is proven by the numerous bones and teeth found in caves, buried in gravel and other deposits.

THE LEOPARD

(*Felis pardus*)

Ingwe of Swazis, Zulus, and Amaxosa : Inkwi of Basuto
(*Kirby*)

THIS well-known and much-dreaded carnivorous animal is generally known in South Africa as a Tiger—*Tijger* or *Vlackte tijger* of the Dutch colonists.

There are, however, no real tigers in this country. The leopard is a very widely spread animal. In fact its distribution is more extensive than any others of the cat family. Wherever forests, kloofs, and rugged bush-covered hills abound, the leopard will be found, unless it should happen to have been exterminated by man. It inhabits Africa from the Cape to the extreme north, and throughout Asia, with the exceptions of Northern Siberia and the high plateau of Thibet. In ancient times it inhabited Europe, for its bones have been found in caverns in Great Britain, Spain, France, and Germany. When our primitive ancestors spread over Europe, they came into conflict with the leopard and dispossessed it of its cave shelters and took

Leopard.

Photo : W. S. Berridge.

possession of them for homes for themselves. In South Africa the leopard is still found haunting the forest-clad parts, but it is slowly but surely being exterminated. In the Cape Province they still give trouble, especially in the forests of the eastern parts of the province, where they issue forth at night and cause much loss to the stock farmers. However, every year they are becoming scarcer, for, when a leopard is in his neighbourhood, the farmer suffers nightly losses of stock, and with trap, poison, dog and gun he wages war against it.

In Southern Rhodesia, leopards are so plentiful that during the year 1910 the Government of the country paid out awards for 250 of these animals, which had been slain in one year.

The leopard is very partial to bush-covered rocky country in the neighbourhood of kloofs and krantzes. When rock crevices or caves are available it makes its home in these if they happen to be in secluded localities not easily discovered by man. Failing such lairs, it takes to the trees or dense matted undergrowth. Occasionally it is found lying concealed in the hollow interior of old forest trees.

It is often met with singly, but more usually in pairs, and sometimes in small family parties of four to six, consisting of the parents and half-grown, and even fully-grown progeny.

The leopard is more cunning, secretive, and treacherous than the lion. Unless forced from its lair it will rarely show itself during the daytime, so thoroughly nocturnal are its habits. When hunger drives, however, it will attack the flocks and herds of the farmer in broad daylight and seize a sheep or goat in the presence of the shepherd and bound off with its victim into the neighbouring scrub. The leopard seldom gives vent to any sound, and when it does, the growl or grunt is merely a low, hoarse, coughing kind of noise.

This animal differs from the lion by reason of its climbing powers, for it is perfectly at home amongst the branches of the forest trees. So silent, cunning, and secretive is it that it can softly steal along a branch and drop upon its unsuspecting prey beneath. Stretching its long and graceful body along the branch of a forest tree overhanging one of the pathways of the bush-dwelling antelopes, it will lie immovable for hours in the hope of securing one of them for a meal.

One evening a friend and I had camped out in a kloof under a large tree and were busy grilling some meat on a fire when, glancing upwards, I saw two large luminous eyes, and presently made out the dark form of a leopard by the fitful light cast by the fire. I sat immovable and stared at those beautiful eyes for about the space of a minute. The leopard lay along a branch quite still, its eyes focussed upon mine. Sliding my hand quietly along the ground I sought to reach my gun, but the animal, observing the movement, turned swiftly

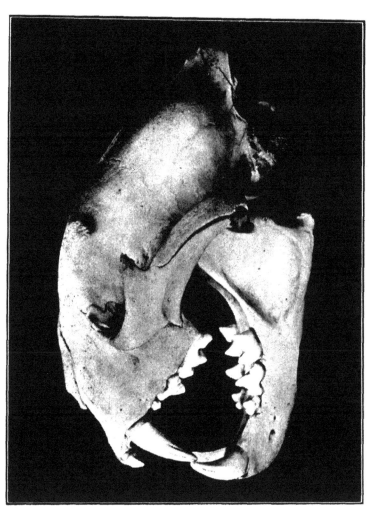

The skull of a Leopard.   Note the powerful canine teeth with which it kills its prey. (Nearly half natural size.)

round on the branch and vanished from sight. On another occasion, when studying birds in their native haunts, I came face to face with another leopard which was also lying stretched full length along a branch about ten feet from the ground. When its eyes and mine met I stood immovable, as, having no weapon other than a stout stick, I reckoned it to be a safer plan than to retreat, as I felt if my earthly career was about to end I might as well have a whack with my cudgel at my slayer. Although within a few paces of the leopard it made no attempt to retreat. I could not detect the slightest movement, not even the winking of an eye. Those great yellow eyes staring down into mine were rather disconcerting. Under such circumstances it is impossible to reckon time, for every second seems an age. Suddenly I flourished my stick and shouted, whereupon the leopard, as on the previous occasion, wheeled round like a pivot on the branch, ran to the root of it, sprang lightly to the ground, and bounded off into the scrub.

The leopard's mission in life is to check many species of animals and birds from overbreeding and upsetting the balance of Nature. We are far too apt to condemn carnivorous animals as cunning, low, bloodthirsty creatures to be killed at sight, and congratulate ourselves on having done an excellent deed. True, the larger carnivora cannot be permitted to exist in the proximity of man, for the reason that they become a pest to him; but away in the wild countries uninhabited by man, or at most, peopled by a few primitive savages, these animals are still fulfilling the mission for which the Creator evolved them.

In rocky districts the leopard preys largely on baboons, and Klip Dassies, otherwise known as Rock Rabbits. In its attacks on the baboons, however, it does not always come off victorious, for instances are known of the old warrior baboons coming to the rescue of one of their number which had been seized by a leopard, and actually tearing it to pieces. An instance is related, in the book entitled *The Monkeyfolk of South Africa*, of a leopard which was attacked by a troop of baboons, as seen by an eyewitness. The leopard waylays the baboons when they are returning to their rocky homes in the krantzes, and often when they are basking on the rocks in the warm sunshine. Stealing up under cover of rocks and scrub, this wily beast springs out upon an unsuspecting baboon, which is invariably a female or a young one, and seizing it, bounds off in an instant into the tangled bush before the leaders of the troop can come to the rescue. If the sleeping-places of these rock-dwelling monkeys should be accessible to the leopard, they have a most uncomfortable time, for, under cover of darkness, this cunning cat steals silently along and drags a screaming victim from its comrades, as it knows full well that baboons are timid and almost helpless during the hours of night.

THE LEOPARD

However, when leopards are known to be in the neighbourhood the baboons seek out the steepest krantz they can find, and find sanctuary at night in crevices in the face of it, for these rock-climbing Chacma Baboons of South Africa can scale the steepest precipices. Previous to the advent of civilised man with his firearms to this country, the leopard was Nature's chief agent in keeping the monkeyfolk from increasing at too rapid a rate.

The Klip Dassie falls a comparatively easy prey to the leopard, which lies concealed amongst the boulders or under some scrub, and when the dassies venture from their retreats in the rock crevices the leopard springs out upon them. A leopard will sometimes lie flattened down for hours near a crevice amongst the rocks on a stony hillside, with paw braced ready to make a drive at the first dassie which may venture forth.

Troops of Vervet Monkeys make their home in the forest districts of South Africa, and the leopard is a source of everlasting terror to them, for he is an adept at climbing, and his ways are so secretive and his tread so light that they are never safe from his attacks. During the hours of darkness they are at his mercy, for, unlike the Chacma Baboon, they cannot climb krantzes to secure a safe retreat. When a leopard is discovered by a troop of Vervet Monkeys, they invariably desert the locality, often travelling considerable distances, for they are well aware that otherwise it is but a matter of time for the whole of the troop to disappear one by one into the capacious stomach of their arch-enemy, which never neglects an opportunity of reducing their numbers and thus fulfilling its mission in life.

In the dense forests and dark, secluded kloofs, far from the habitations of civilised man, the leopard hunts its prey by day as well as by night.

I happened to be the witness of one of those tragedies which occur daily and nightly in the animal world, and which at times make humane men wonder why it was necessary in the evolution of life that in order that one creature may live another's life must be taken. The struggle for the survival of the fittest is indeed a terrible and relentless one in the lower animal world. I was lying concealed in some dense scrub watching with field-glasses the antics of a troop of Vervet Monkeys, on a low branch of an old forest giant, the top of which was covered with a dense growth of creepers which had pushed their way up from the ground to light and life. Presently I observed a large yellow body drop like a stone from the dense foliage at the top of the tree, and next instant the monkeys, chattering and screaming in abject terror, vanished amid the surrounding bushes. A leopard had dropped down in the midst of several monkeys on a branch, and striking out fiercely, it succeeded in hooking two of them with the large curved claws of its fore limbs, and with its victims it fell with

A Leopard at bay on the trunk ot a tree.

a thud to the ground, and holding one of the monkeys down with a paw, bit the other through the back. Rising, it looked around and listened intently. Satisfying itself that no foe was near, it squatted down cat fashion and leisurely ate one of its victims, ever and anon raising its head and shoulders to listen and glance around. Picking the other victim up in its jaws it calmly walked off into the forest with it. Such is an instance of tragedies which occur every moment of time in the lower animal world.

Some people consider it distinctly cruel to deprive animals of their liberty, although they may be confined in large, roomy, comfortable cages and all their physical needs provided for. Such folk know little or nothing of the hardships which most animals in their native haunts are called upon to undergo in the shape of scarcity of food, inclement weather, and the necessity to be at all times on their guard against the many enemies by which they are surrounded. The feelings of the lower animals cannot be gauged by those of us who have the mental, moral and spiritual faculties in an advanced condition of development. If the physical needs of the lower animals, and even the primitive races of men, are provided for, they are then in a condition of perfect happiness, like the yokel who was lazily swinging on a farm gate and chewing a bit of bacon. Asked what was the greatest happiness he could think of, he said, " Swinging on a gate and plenty of bacon." In the Eastern Transvaal the rodent known as the Cane Rat, which is an animal of about the size of a full-grown rabbit, is a favourite food of the leopard. In cultivated fields and in the sugar plantations along the coast of Natal these Cane Rats do considerable mischief.

Most of the denizens of kloof, mountain and forest are preyed upon by the leopard, chief amongst which are the Bush Bucks, Duiker Bucks, and Bush Pigs.

Guinea fowls, Francolins, and others of the larger birds are welcome additions to the diet of this great beast.

Should a leopard dash amongst a troop of monkeys, a family of wild pigs, &c., it slays right and left, and apparently kills for the mere sake of taking life. This in reality is not so. Carnivorous animals, unlike those which subsist on vegetation, have not a regular supply of food assured them, and for days at a time are obliged to fast or satisfy their hunger in a most unsatisfactory way on small creatures which at other times they disdain. Consequently when the chance offers they slay in a wholesale manner, and if not molested or alarmed will usually return nightly until all the victims are devoured, for most of the carnivora will eat flesh even when putrid. Some carnivorous animals carefully carry away and hide what meat they cannot devour on the spot. A rather remarkable custom of the leopard in South Africa is that of carrying its

A Leopard at bay in thorny scrub.

This leopard was blackish in colour, and the typical black spots were very indistinct on the body and quite absent on the head.

. THE LEOPARD

victim up a tree and fixing it securely in a fork. The object is twofold; the leopard, like some of our own species, prefers its venison in an odoriferous condition, when it is in a mood for dining; and secondly, it knows full well that if the carcase was left to lie upon the ground, a host of sneaking jackals, wild dogs, or other carnivorous animals would quickly eat it up.

Before the advent of the men of the Stone Age, the leopard had no enemies in South Africa which it had much cause to fear. True, it was no match for the lion, but it was always careful not to invite that formidable beast to attack it. The Hunting Leopard or Chita it did not fear, for, although fleet of foot, this animal had not the strength of the leopard, or such efficient weapons of offence and defence.

Leopards were reduced in numbers chiefly by the males slaying one another in battle, for they will fight to the death for a mate, or in defence of their favourite hunting grounds.

In its attacks on the porcupine the leopard occasionally finds its match. An instance occurred of a too venturesome or inexperienced leopard meeting its death by getting several porcupine quills firmly imbedded in its tongue and palate; and another which, when shot, was noticed to have a swollen and suppurating foot caused by the presence of a porcupine quill which had penetrated deep into the pad. In the former instance the leopard had evidently attempted to seize a porcupine with its jaws, and in the latter case a blow had no doubt been aimed at a porcupine's most vulnerable part, viz. its head, and unfortunately for the leopard, instead of striking the snout of the intended victim, its soft pad struck the sharp point of a quill.

It is a common occurrence for hunters to have their meat purloined by leopards during the night. So wary and secretive is the animal that it frequently succeeds in actually carrying off the meat without waking the dogs, and the dogs of hunters are by no means slothful or inclined to sleep heavily.

Instances are on record of it having even crept into tents and taken the flesh from beside the sleeping men, the evidence of the fact being the disappearance of the provender and the spoor of the animal.

When the men of the Stone Age penetrated into South Africa from the north, driven down by hordes stronger than themselves, or in search of better hunting grounds, they attacked the leopard, and driving it forth from the rock shelters and caves, took possession of them. However, the leopard had comparatively little to fear from these wild men. On the advent of the pygmy Bushmen the leopard had a more formidable enemy to contend with.

In pairs and in hordes these pygmies stalked the

leopard, and getting within a dozen paces or so, would discharge their bone-tipped arrows, the points of which were inoculated with a deadly poison. The leopard, feeling the prick of the arrow point through its skin, would bite viciously at the smarting wound, and possibly take no further heed until the poison had done its deadly work. Then, from out of their place of conceal-ment, the little yellow men would steal forth, and with sharp-edged stone flakes quickly remove the skin, which subsequently would be worn as a trophy.

If a Bushman succeeded in wounding a leopard with an arrow, and should it bound off into the forest, he slowly and cautiously followed its spoor, accompanied by several of his comrades, knowing full well he would sooner or later find the animal lying in a more or less paralysed condition, if not actually dead.

On the advent of the Bantu tribes, the leopard had a more intelligent and stronger enemy, who, for mutual protection, combined and hunted it from its lairs with dogs, and slew it with spears, for these Bantu people owned flocks and herds which fell an easy prey to the prowling leopard.

The efforts of the Kafirs, however, did not diminish the number of these animals to any appreciable degree, and finding the stock of the natives an easier prey than antelopes, the leopards levied a heavy toll, compelling the exasperated owners to herd up their cattle by night in kraals adjacent to their huts, and to carefully guard them during the daytime when out grazing.

Even so, the leopard frequently succeeded in carrying lambs, sheep, goats, and calves away unobserved, or before the shepherd could come to the rescue. Driven to despair, the angry natives would turn out in their hundreds, armed with large skin shields, spears, and kerries, and hunt down and slay the beast which robbed them of what they valued almost better than life itself.

It was not until the advent of the European colonist with his firearms that the leopard met his master. However, even so the fight was a long and arduous one, and to-day this wary, cunning, and secretive cat manages not only to elude the hunter in even the settled portions of the country, but actually succeeds in levying a heavy toll on his sheep, goats, calves, ostriches, and poultry. When hunted with dogs the leopard usually takes refuge in a tree, and is then easily shot. If a river bars its way to safety, it does not hesitate to plunge in, for it is an excellent swimmer. When cornered or wounded the leopard will turn viciously upon and charge its tormentors with the greatest of fury, courage, and determination. Many cases are on record of hunters being mauled and killed in this way. Often the leopard will charge into the midst of a pack of dogs and in the space of a few moments kill and maim half a dozen or more. In South Africa man-eating leopards are unknown, but in India many instances are recorded.

Unlike most other animals, the leopard has no instinctive dread of dogs, for throughout India it has the reputation of swooping down whenever a chance presents itself, by night and by day, and carrying off dogs from the very presence of their owners.

In South Africa this trait is not so pronounced, although it is a fairly common occurrence for the dogs of natives, and even those of European hunters, to be carried off in the night and devoured.

A pointer dog belonging to a friend was carried off one night by a leopard. We had only extinguished the light in the lantern about five minutes, and were composing ourselves to rest under a tarpaulin-covered wagon, when we were startled into alertness by the sharp terrified bark of a dog, followed by a succession of abject yelps, and lastly a muffled squall. The other dogs, yelping in the extremity of their terror, dashed into our presence and crouched on our blankets. Lighting the lantern and seizing our weapons we cautiously sallied forth, and presently discovered splashes of blood on the ground and herbage, and also the spoor of a leopard.

A gentleman living at Siussi, in German East Africa, has recently written the following interesting account of a battle between a python and a leopard : " I was sitting at breakfast with one of my friends, when suddenly a native servant rushed into the dining-room and informed me that a fight was going on between a snake and a leopard. When we got outside we saw the awful but exciting battle between the two—a full-grown leopard was encircled by a giant snake. The leopard tried to free itself from the snake by biting and striking it, but the living circle became smaller and smaller. The snake beat the earth fiercely with each bite and blow from the leopard, and its shiny skin hung torn all over it, but it did not spare its strength. The leopard seemed lost, but when the snake for a moment relaxed its grip, the leopard stretched itself out, and, with a final effort, bit the snake in its left jaw. One could hear the bones being crushed. The severely wounded snake beat about it a few more times with its tail, and made a final attempt to encircle the leopard, but its strength was gone— a few more twitches and it was done. But what was the condition of the victor? Deadly tired, with broken bones, it lay there looking at us and grinding its teeth. It endeavoured to rid itself of the snake, but had also to give up the struggle. We gave it the *coup de grâce*. The stripped snake-skin measured six and three-quarter yards in length, and three-quarters of a yard in breadth."

Books of adventure and sport teem with accounts of encounters with leopards, all of which go to show that when wounded and hard pressed it is even more to be feared than the lion.

An African Python (*Python sebae*). This snake attains a length of
at least 20 feet. It kills it prey by constriction.

THE LEOPARD

When captured young the leopard is easily tamed, and may be handled freely. It is taught to perform in circuses, and is one of the typical show animals of travelling menageries and zoological gardens. It is capable of considerable training, but is invariably more or less morose and sullen.

When attacking its prey, if it be large, the leopard seizes it by the throat, buries its powerful claws in the creature's neck, and either breaks the backbone or strangles it with vicious bites with its powerful jaws, which are armed with sharp and strong canine teeth.

The tiger starts eating its victim hindquarters first; the leopard, on the contrary, tears open the abdomen, drags out the contents, and feeds first upon the lungs, liver, heart, kidneys, and a portion of the intestines.

The number of leopard cubs at a birth in this country is usually three, although as many as six are recorded. The cubs are born, as a general rule, during the months of October, November, and December.

Leopards differ considerably in size and markings. The colour of the fur of the typical leopard is yellow of varying shades, profusely covered with rosette-shaped black markings. These markings and the general body colour vary according to the part of the country inhabited by the animal. In Asia some leopards are quite black, and even in

South Africa these black varieties have been recorded. There is a difference, however, in the Asiatic and the South African black leopards. In the former the body colour, instead of being yellow, is black, and the rosettes may be seen standing out, owing to their greater degree of blackness, like spots on watered silk when the light shines obliquely upon it. In the African variety of black leopard the blackness is caused by a profusion of black spots, which fuse and sometimes present an almost uniform black coat.

When I first took over the management of the Port Elizabeth Museum, I found a black leopard on exhibition, which had been shot in Humansdorp district. At a distance the body appeared almost black, yet, when closely viewed, the rosettes, although fusing with their neighbours, did not obliterate the usual yellow body colour entirely. The head and neck of this specimen showed more yellow than the body. Unfortunately the skin was found to be riddled by insect pests, and had to be destroyed, with the exception of the head and a portion of the neck.

THE SERVAL CAT

(*Felis serval*)

Also known as the Tiger Bush Cat (Tijger-bosch-kat):
Indhloti of Zulus and Swazis (*Kirby*); Indhlozi of
Amaxosa (*Stanford*); Tali of Bechuanas; Tlodi of
Basutos (*Kirby*).

THE Serval inhabits the whole of Africa, but is
commonest in the southern portion of the continent. Wherever there is sufficient cover and an
abundance of the animals and birds on which it
feeds, there you will find the Serval.

It is often met with on the open plains and
hillsides where the grass grows long and coarse,
but it is more partial to the reedy and bush-covered
banks of streams, where food in the shape of small
mammals and water-birds is plentiful.

In South Africa the Serval inhabits the bush-
veld, and when much persecuted by man it retires
to the dense forests, and seldom shows itself outside
its leafy home. In Natal I usually found the
Serval in dark wooded kloofs, and in the dense
scrub on the sides of hills and along the banks of
rivers. I have never yet met with it out upon the

grassy veld, except in the vicinity of bushy cover, into which it always raced when startled.

It is a night prowler by habit, and rests during the day in the midst of masses of undergrowth or in whatever suitable cover the nature of its habitat affords. I have frequently found it on the branches or in the hollow interiors of large forest trees.

The Serval is remarkable for its fleetness, but, like the Chita, it cannot keep up a high degree of speed for long. It progresses in great bounds, often springing clear of the long grass and stubbly bushes. It is strictly carnivorous, and in South Africa it levies a heavy toll upon the smaller bush antelopes, Tree Dassies, and various kinds of rodent animals. Birds both large and small, as well as their young, fall victims to this active cat.

Although the Serval destroys considerable numbers of game animals and birds, yet it performs excellent service for man in destroying rats, mice, and that destructive animal known as the " Cane Rat," which scientifically is not a rat at all.

In the wild condition the Serval is shy, timid, and secretive, and rarely shows itself by day unless driven forth from its lair by dogs. In these cases it invariably takes refuge in a tree, and remains at bay, snarling and hissing. So excessively timid is this cat that one day when walking in a forest in Natal I disturbed one of them in the act of chasing a little Blue Buck. My terrier dog gave chase, and the cat, in the extremity of its terror,

The Serval (*Felis serval*) making his spring. The Africander
people call him Tijger-bosch-kat or Tijger-kat ; the Amaxosa
people, Indhlozi ; the Zulus and Swazis, Indhloti ; the Basutos,
Tlodi; and the Bechuanas, Tali.

sprang up a tree and showed the greatest alarm, hissing and snarling with excessive energy in the hope, evidently, of scaring us off. I approached and cast a stone at it, whereupon it rapidly ran along a branch, dropped to the ground, and bolted full speed, outdistancing the dog in a few moments.

In the wilder, forest-covered parts where man rarely penetrates, the Serval may often be seen abroad during the daytime on the watch for monkeys and birds.

I had two Servals in captivity for a number of years. One of these was captured when almost adult, and in spite of the greatest of patience and gentleness I could not manage to tame it. A Kafir boy of about fourteen years of age cleaned out the cage every day, and on one occasion prodded and otherwise teased this Serval with his broom, whereupon the cat sprang upon him with a snarl of anger and severely lacerated his face and neck with its claws and teeth. The other Serval was captured in the kittenhood stage, and grew up as tame as any domestic cat. I was obliged to keep it confined most of the time, either on a chain or in a large cage, owing to its fondness for my poultry and pigeons. Now and then I took it for a walk out upon the veld, and gave it its liberty. On calling out its name, " Foxey," it would instantly gallop back to me and affectionately rub its head against my leg. Nothing delighted it more than to be allowed to hunt in the grass for rats and mice,

It disturbed a covey of partridges one day, and with a leap it secured one in the air, six feet from the ground. I once saw it make a most remarkable leap. It happened to observe a Bush Pigeon sitting on a branch, and crouching low it took advantage of the scrubby bushes for cover, and succeeded in crawling unseen almost beneath the spot where the bird was preening its plumage. Then, with a single bound, the Serval leaped straight up into the air, a distance of about ten feet, seized the bird with its claws, and fell in a heap on the ground with its prey.

The degree of celerity with which this cat could bound up the perpendicular trunk of a tree was marvellous. When rambling in the bush-veld with this tame Serval, we surprised a Bush Dassie on the ground. It at once scurried up a tree, but the cat was after it in a moment, and seemed to actually run up the trunk of the tree and seize the dassie before it could reach the hole at the top which communicated with the hollow interior. The moment it seized its victim, it fell with a thud to the ground, fearful lest the struggling dassie should escape from its jaws.

One day my Zulu servant, in my absence, took upon himself to take " Foxey " for a ramble, and succeeded in losing her in a neighbouring forest. He told me she gave chase to a buck, and although he searched everywhere he failed to find her. Much vexed at the loss of my special pet, I informed

This is " Foxey," the author's tame Serval.

him I would " break his neck " if he didn't find her. Of course I didn't mean it, but he evidently thought I did, for he disappeared. I learned on inquiry he had taken his blanket, sleeping mat, tin billy, and some mealie meal and salt, and had gone off. Thinking he had deserted, as is so usual with Kafirs, I thought no more about him. Two days later he turned up, leading my beloved cat by a chain. With a proud smile, which showed his gleaming white teeth to perfection, the Zulu said that for two days he wandered through the forest calling aloud the cat's name. Dispirited and sad he sat down by a stream and solaced himself with snuff. Rising once again he made the forest ring with " Foxey," and to his delight the object of his search bounded from some adjacent reeds and showed her joy in the most extravagant leaps, rollings, and purrings. On sighting me she sprang forward, jerking the chain from the Kafir's grasp, and nearly scrubbed holes in my trousers, so hard and so persistently did she rub her head in characteristic cat fashion against my legs.

Foxey conceived a great affection for the kitten of a domestic cat. It seemed the little mite was left an orphan at an early age, owing to its mother being bitten by a venomous snake, and perishing miserably. The little creature would mew and scrub its nose and body against the fine wire mesh of the Serval's cage. The latter at first made rather frantic efforts to get at the kitten, and it was quite apparent she would instantly have killed it if she had been able to get a grip of it. However the wee mite continued to make friendly advances, and lay for hours close against the wire netting of the cage. Foxey very soon responded to these overtures of affection and love, as do practically all animals, and it was very touching to see the great cat and the tiny kitten trying to rub their noses together and carry on a conversation. The two would lie as near each other as the wire side of the cage would allow; and at other times they endeavoured to play, darting at one another and leaping and capering.

Being quite satisfied the kitten would come to no harm, I took it with me inside Foxey's cage and gently laid it down. Foxey instantly advanced and made the most extravagant demonstrations, leaping and springing around and over the kitten. She then began to purr most energetically, and lying down, licked the kitten very gently and rubbed it with her nose in token of love and friendship. The kitten was equally demonstrative, and showed by its actions it was greatly pleased.

After a time, thinking it best to take the little mite away, I stooped to pick it up, but the Serval instantly seized it with her teeth by the loose skin of the back of its neck, in the way a mother carries her kittens, and retiring into her kennel she threw a protecting paw around it and hissed loudly and threateningly when I approached. However, al-

" Foxey " the Serval, and her friends.

though she showed great displeasure when I forcibly took the kitten away, she did not attempt to bite or scratch me. After this the kitten gave us no peace. It simply haunted Foxey's cage, and when any of us made an appearance it clamoured most frantically for admittance. Its desire was invariably gratified, for I noticed that the Serval was now always happy and contented. Previously, when alone, she crooned and called almost incessantly until some of us came to her. So long as I was in sight she was happy and content. I used in my spare time to take a book and an easy-chair and sit against the wire side of her cage, reading. At these times she would always lie contentedly as close to me as she could get, and whenever I took any notice of her she would immediately show her pleasure by purring.

It has been stated the Serval cannot be fully tamed. This is not so, for Foxey was as tame and docile as any domestic cat. When full-grown she did not lose any of her playfulness, and nothing gave her keener joy than when I romped and played with her. Grabbing me round the leg she would grip tight and pretend to bite, then letting go she would scurry around in circles, awaiting a chance to rush in.

I used to chain her up at times inside a wire-netting enclosure. The netting was for the purpose of keeping off the fowls. The old rooster knew to an inch the length of Foxey's chain, and poking his head through the wire mesh he retrieved sundry scraps of food from her dish, or bits which had got scattered. One day Foxey's food dish was about a foot in distance from the fence, and the cock, watching his chance, poked his head through the wire and snapped up scraps from the dish. The cat made several leaps at intervals at the thief, but finding that her chain jerked her back each time, she sat down and deliberated. Presently she took up a position as close to the dish as her chain would allow, and closing her eyes she pretended to sleep. Her forepaws were innocently doubled up under her chest, and she seemed indifferent to all outward concerns. The old rooster eyed her suspiciously for quite a long while. Then he made a pretence to peck at the dish. He repeated this manœuvre a dozen or more times. Evidently being satisfied the cat was really asleep, he grabbed a morsel from the dish, chuckled audibly, and gulped it down. Again and yet again he did the same thing, when, like a lightning flash, the cat's long paw shot out, and next instant the cock's headless body was tumbling about outside the fence. The Serval had struck her claws deep into the head of the fowl, and retracting her paw like the recoil of stretched rubber, the head was jerked from the body.

On another occasion I had her confined in a large aviary. In the same cage was the other Serval already mentioned, which was a male, and now adult. When in the act of opening the top half of the door to renew the water in the drinking-vessel, a servant came from an outhouse and cast a dish of grain upon the ground behind me for the pigeons and fowls. The sight· of the pigeons flying down, and the poultry gobbling up the food, was too much for those cats, and while I was bending down to reach for the dish both cats leap-frogged over my back and played havoc with the poultry. Shouting to the servant to hold back the spring door of the aviary, I seized Foxey and hurled her through the small doorway, and then the other. The latter was a powerful and savage beast, and never before had been handled, but so intent was it on worrying the life out of a fowl that it hadn't time to think of turning on me when in desperation I grasped it by the loose skin of its back.

I endeavoured to wean these two cats on to a diet of bread and porridge and milk, with a weekly supply of meat. Although they always ate up their food greedily they did not thrive, for it brought on a condition of chronic diarrhœa, which persisted until I again fed them on meat only. Their gastric and intestinal juices were not of a nature to digest starchy foods, and digestive and intestinal disturbances were consequently induced.

The Serval when in the vicinity of man is a pest, by reason of its fondness for poultry, young ostriches, kids, and lambs, and the farmer does his best to exterminate it in his neighbourhood.

During buck hunts, when the bush is beaten by crowds of natives, these Serval Cats often break cover and are shot.

The male Serval has a more massive head than the female, as well as a better developed body. When cornered by dogs it fights fiercely and grimly to the last, and usually succeeds in either killing or severely mauling some of its assailants.

I once saw a mongrel dog disembowelled by a Serval. The cat had been pursued and surrounded by a dozen or more dogs, and in the excitement one of them rushed in at it. In an instant the cat had the dog by the throat, and throwing it down it at the same time cast itself upon its side and with a tremendous stroke tore open the abdomen of its victim with its hind claws.

The Serval, although so widespread, is nowhere common. This is somewhat surprising, for it has no enemies in the lower animal kingdom which deliberately hunt it down with the intention of taking its life. The lion, leopard, and chita do not interfere with it unless it should be foolish enough to bother them when devouring their prey. The wild-cat tribe do not hunt and kill other carnivorous or flesh-eating animals for food unless forced by starvation.

When two male Servals are placed in the same cage they fight to the death, unless reared together from kittenhood.

In the wild condition, on the approach of the

A female Serval (*Felis serval*) on the bank of a dry river. The male is more robust than the female. The Serval is as large as a Pointer Dog.

breeding season, the males become very aggressive in their demeanour to one another, and fight most desperately, and in this way numbers are destroyed. These cats are all very jealous of their hunting-grounds, and bitterly resent the intrusion of others of their kind, knowing instinctively that their food supply would soon become exhausted should too many of them live in proximity. The chief factors, no doubt, in checking the too rapid increase of carnivorous animals are epidemics of disease and starvation, for it is obvious that if the flesh-eating animals in any district unduly increase in numbers, the animals which furnish their food supply diminish proportionately. Should famishing car-nivorous animals invade other parts of the country, they usually find them already occupied by those of their kind, and these strongly resist the invasion of their game preserves. It is simply a matter of self-preservation, and their destructive passions are at once aroused. This instinct, if we can term it such, is widespread, and even embraces the human species, for past history shows that of all things which men resented most, it was the invasion by others of a different tribe or nation of the territories which they had grown up to regard as their own. This is a wise provision of Nature, for the first step in both physical and mental degeneration is overcrowding. Should this occur, in spite of Nature's efforts to prevent it, epidemics of disease break out and sweep off the surplus, and once again the balance is restored. The Serval once seen is never forgotten, for it is so different in its markings and shape to others of the cat tribe. It possesses a somewhat slender body and long legs, which give it a lanky appearance. Its tail is comparatively short; its fur is fulvous or tawny reddish-yellow, profusely covered with black spots. In height it is nearly two feet at the shoulder; its body from nose to tail is three feet, and the tail is a foot long.

Black specimens of Serval Cats are occasionally seen. These, however, are abnormal. Like the black varieties of the leopard, the body colour is dull blackish, and in certain lights the spots can be seen standing out darker. The normal yellow colour of the fur varies occasionally more or less, some specimens being of a deeper reddish-yellow than others.

THE BLACK-FOOTED CAT

(*Felis nigripes*)

Kakikaan of Bechuanas (*Burchell*); Tsipa by natives of Kalahari Desert (*Livingstone*)

THE Black-footed Cat is so called because the soles of the fore and hind limbs are black. This cat is in general appearance like a dwarf Serval. It is an inhabitant of Bechuanaland and the Kalahari, but is evidently rather scarce, for few museums

An adult Black-footed Cat (*Felis nigripes*) and a kitten of the same species. These cats are similar in point of size to average domestic cats. Its buff colour and black spots blend perfectly with the nature of the ground and semi-dry vegetation of its habitat.

possess examples, and hunters in the parts of the country inhabited by it seldom mention having observed it. Occasionally skins are seen forming portions of karosses made by the Bechuana natives. The Black-footed Cat is in size similar to an adult domestic cat, and its description is as follows: Pale sandy or buff, becoming lighter on the throat and under parts. Sides profusely marked with black irregular spots, which on the shoulder and neck run together into stripes. Top of the head dark, caused by an abundance of short close brown hairs. Cheeks paler, with two blackish streaks. Legs with three black rings more or less well defined. Soles of fore and hind feet black; hence the name of Black-footed Cat. Tail comparatively short, spotted and tipped with black. Length of head and body, 20 to 22 inches. Tail, 6 inches.

When captured in the kittenhood stage this cat, if kindly treated, becomes as tame as any of the domestic breed of cat, and will not attempt to wander away from the homestead if allowed its liberty, provided, of course, it is taken into captivity when very small.

I obtained a kitten from Bechuanaland, but it was two months old when captured, and although it became tame and allowed me to stroke it, yet when I allowed it its liberty it instantly made for the nearest cover in a crouching secretive attitude. The colour of the Black-footed Cat blends perfectly with its dry, buff-coloured surroundings, so much so that it is invisible at a few paces distant when crouching low, as it often does, evidently well aware that so long as it remains immovable it will, in all likelihood, be passed by unobserved.

THE AFRICAN WILD CAT

(*Felis ocreata caffra*)

Also known as the Kafir Cat, Bull Head, Wild Cat, Graauw-kat, Imbodhla, Ingada, and Impaka

THE African Wild Cat inhabits the whole of Africa from the Cape to the Mediterranean, and extends to South-western Asia, viz. Syria and Arabia. It also still exists in Sardinia.

In South Africa this cat is common in the bush-veld and forests, and in fact wherever there is any suitable cover and an abundance of prey.

Although in South Africa the Wild Cat has been found to differ slightly from its kind beyond the Zambesi, the difference is by no means sufficient to justify us in making a distinct species of it, so we merely regard it as a distinct local race, and distinguish it from the others by making what is termed a sub-species of it, and naming it *Felis ocreata caffra.*

In South Africa the Wild Cat, when living in the neighbourhood of human habitations, rarely shows itself during the daytime, hiding away in the midst of dense brushwood, clefts amongst the

An African Wild Cat and her kittens. The speckled greyish-brown colour with irregular black cross markings of this cat blend perfectly with the grass and other foliage.

rocks, and high up on the branches of great forest trees, or in cavities in the trunks.

Many a time I have surprised the Wild Cat in the bush-veld during the daytime on the prowl for food. At other times, when climbing forest trees to inspect the contents of birds' nests, I have startled this cat from its lair on a large horizontal branch, or at the crown of the trunk of an old tree, and sometimes from the interior of a large bird's nest. I surprised one of them in the nest of a Hammer Head or Hammerkop (*Scopus umbretta*). These birds build enormous nests of twigs, &c., sometimes big enough to fill a Scotch cart. The entrance hole is at the side, and the interior chamber is lined with mud. Bringing my face parallel with the aperture, I was greeted with a quick succession of spitting hisses, and before I could recover my presence of mind, a Wild Cat sprang forth, clawed my felt hat from my head, fell to the ground, and vanished into the undergrowth.

Many a time my terriers have hunted these cats out of the tangled brushwood, or located them in crevices amongst rocks.

When alarmed, they trot along in a crouching attitude, endeavouring to escape observation, exactly after the manner of domestic cats. When actually chased they make off at a gallop, but are easily overtaken by dogs. When hard pressed they bound up a tree and endeavour to conceal themselves amongst the foliage.

When brought to bay the Wild Cat fights fiercely and is game to the last. When pursued, and if no trees are within reach, it takes refuge in rock crevices and down the burrows of the ant-eater. This cat is extremely strong and active for its size, and attacks the young of the smaller antelopes, and easily overpowers adult Blue Duikers. Hares, Bush Dassies, Klip Dassies, game birds, bush birds and their nestlings, rats, mice, and a host of other creatures fall a prey to it.

The Wild Cat is a pest to the stock and poultry-keeper. If one of these cats is in the vicinity, and should it discover the roosting-place of the fowls, it pays nightly visits to them until all are devoured.

A Dutch farmer friend in Natal possessed a specially fine lot of turkeys which roosted at night in a tree near the homestead. One morning he found three lying dead at the foot of the tree; choice morsels having been eaten out of each. Removing two, he baited a steel spring trap with the third, and succeeded in capturing a large male Wild Cat.

These cats do not confine their attention to poultry only. Young ostriches, lambs, and kids are also killed and devoured by them. In captivity the Wild Cat prefers fresh untainted meat, indicating that in the wild state it hunts and kills its own food, and does not relish carrion.

Should a Wild Cat be in the neighbourhood of a farm, and if it has started to interfere with poultry or stock, the farmer must at once exert himself to destroy the marauder, as he will have no peace while it remains alive, for it will haunt the place so long as a meal is obtainable. Fortunately, unlike the jackal, it is easily trapped or poisoned. If it should kill a kid or lamb, it satisfies its appetite on the carcase and returns to its lair, but comes back the following night to feast on the remains of its victim. Sometimes a single Wild Cat will slay a dozen fowls in a night. It eats a little of the tenderest flesh from several, or else carries one of the victims off and leaves the rest untouched.

So closely is the African Wild Cat related to the common domestic cat that it breeds freely with it. Large numbers of domestic cats in South Africa are the offspring of wild tom cats and domestic female cats. In fact when Wild Cats are in the neighbourhood it is usually impossible to keep domestic tom cats, for their wild cousins, being stronger and superior in fighting powers, soon succeed in killing them off. These quarrels occur during the breeding season.

I frequently stayed at the farm of a Dutch friend in Natal, and his cats often gave birth to kittens which were almost pure-bred Wild Cats. His cats for a period of ten years or more had interbred with the wild species, which are common in the vicinity of the homestead, and the domestic strain was practically bred out.

A tom cat of his, which was at least two-thirds of the Wild Cat breed, was found on the stoep one morning in a dying condition, having been severely mauled, no doubt, by a wild rival of superior strength. Several farmer friends in the uplands of Natal possessed domestic cats which had all the markings of the wild species. In fact I knew an animal dealer who was in the habit of purchasing these domestic cats and disposing of them to Continental zoos as being tamed African Wild Cats. African Wild Cats are specially interesting for the reason that they were held sacred by the ancient Egyptians, who made a practice of embalming their bodies when they died. Tremendous numbers of these mummy cats have been discovered at Bubalis and Beni-Hassan, which clearly shows that the Egyptians of four thousand and more years ago had succeeded in domesticating the African Wild Cat. Although there is some difference of opinion over the matter, it can without much fear of contradiction be taken for granted that the present-day European cats originated from these African Wild Cats.

The fact that the females of the domestic cats readily mate and breed with these Wild Cats in South Africa is very significant in this connection. It must not be assumed, however, that all varieties of domestic cats have originated entirely from the African Wild Cat. Domestic cats would, for instance, in all likelihood interbreed with the European

A pair of African Wild Cats at home. Their colour tones perfectly with that of the ground, the rocks, and undergrowth.

Wild Cat ; and in India a blending would no doubt occur with the native wild cats of that country. In fact there are strong reasons for assuming that the domestic cats of India originated in the wild cats of that country, and in recent times inter-blended with those from the west, whose progenitors were African Wild Cats.

From the evidence of rock paintings and etchings, the ancient Egyptians were in the habit of training domesticated Wild Cats to capture game birds, and probably small mammals as well.

The usual custom, evidently, was to embark in a boat with some decoy birds and a trained cat or two, and to proceed to the shallows abounding in papyrus reeds, where waterfowl of various kinds congregated in great numbers. The cat was trained to capture the birds for its master. One is depicted in an Egyptian painting, which shows it in the act of holding a bird in its mouth, another under its forepaws, and a third between its hind feet. The cat was also, no doubt, trained to retrieve birds from the water, which had been maimed or killed by the fowler. If the cats of those times had as strong a dislike for water as those of to-day, considerable patience must have been required in their training to overcome this natural repugnance to water, although cats, when hard pressed, will plunge into a stream and swim across.

On these fowling expeditions with their trained

cats, the ancient Egyptians also collected the eggs and young of the waterfowl for food.

The African Wild Cat has from two to four kittens at a birth, as a general rule. These are usually born in cavities amongst rocks; in the midst of dense tangled undergrowth; down deserted ant-eater holes, or in the hollow interior of an old forest tree.

At Perseverance, near Port Elizabeth, a female Wild Cat was killed by dogs, and two kittens were discovered in the centre of a creeper-covered thorn-bush. It was during the month of October, and the kittens were about two months old at the time. On another occasion an adult male Wild Cat was killed and sent to the Port Elizabeth Museum. It was a partial albino, being about two-thirds white. It was, unfortunately, in too decomposed a condition to preserve.

The Wild Cat is in size similar to a rather over-grown domestic cat, such as is seen in butchers' shops at times. The male is more robust in ap-pearance than the female. The prevailing colour is speckled greyish-brown. The base of the fur is dark slate, yellowish in the centre, and the tip of each hair is ringed black and white. On the underparts these rings are absent, consequently those parts are yellowish.

The fur along the ridge of the back is blackish, and in most specimens the body is striped with brown irregular bands, which on the upper parts of the legs are black. The degree of intensity of these bands or stripes varies considerably. In the kittens the transverse stripes are very pronounced and black in colour. The tail is distinctly ringed and tipped with black. In the female the darker markings are not so distinct, and the body colour is somewhat lighter than in the male.

THE CARACAL

(Felis caracal)

Also known as the Lynx, Rooi-kat, Persian Lynx, Incawa
of the Amaxosa, and Tuane of the Bechuanas

In South Africa the Caracal is better known as the
Lynx or Rooi-kat (Red Cat). The three names by
which it is known are all significant of some peculiarity in the animal. The word Caracal is derived
from the Turkish, meaning " Black-eared," because
of the backs of its ears and tufts of hair in their
tips being black. In Persia and India it is known
as the " Siyah-gush," which also has the same
meaning as the word Caracal.

Rooi or Red Cat is also an appropriate name, for
this animal, with the exception of the backs of its
ears and the ear tufts, is uniform brick red in colour.

The Caracal is not a true Lynx, but it so closely
resembles it that none but the experienced zoo-
logist would recognise the difference. The Caracal
is the link between the typical cats and lynxes. The
chief difference between the Caracal and true Lynx
is that the latter has a shorter tail, a ruff around
the throat, and thicker fur than the former.

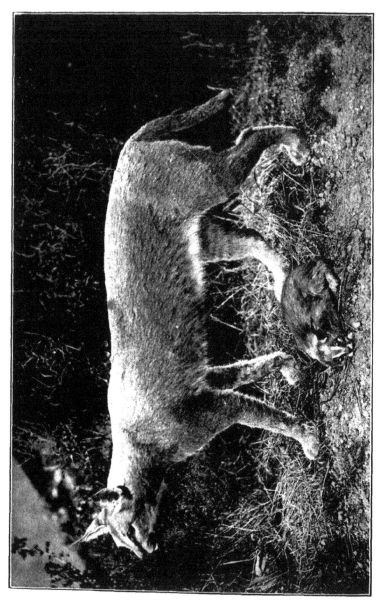

An adult Caracal, otherwise known as a Rooi-kat and Lynx. Also a kitten of the same species. An adult is as large as a Collie Dog.

THE CARACAL

The Caracal is found from the Cape right through Africa to its most northern limits, and extends eastwards to Arabia, Persia, and the western parts of India. In the Knysna and Addo forests, near Port Elizabeth, this cat, although not actually common, is sufficiently so to be regarded as a pest. During the past six years over a score have been shot and sent to me, and it is a common occurrence for farmers to shoot, trap, and poison them. As many as a dozen have, during the past four years, to my knowledge, been captured alive in the Uitenhage district.

In the past in South Africa the Rooi-kat inhabited the open country, such as the sparsely-wooded bush-veld, and was frequently met with in the more exposed kloofs, on thinly-wooded hillsides, and amongst tall grass and reeds. Except in the wilder secluded parts of the country, where the European with his gun and dogs rarely penetrates, this large and wary cat has now taken to the dense forests and thickly-wooded kloofs and scrub-covered hillsides. From these secure retreats it issues forth by night into the more open country in search of some bird or animal for a meal. Its natural diet consists of the smaller antelopes, Klip Dassies, Tree Dassies, hares, rats, and other mammals, as well as the larger birds. If its natural prey should prove insufficient for its needs, or should the wild animals and birds have become shy and experienced, and consequently difficult to stalk and capture, it levies a heavy toll on the stock farmer, attacking his sheep, goats, calves, young ostriches, and poultry. Should a flock of sheep or goats be within convenient distance of its lair, it will not hesitate to venture forth in broad day-light and attack them. Should a shepherd make his appearance it instantly bounds off and vanishes in the thick bush, where, as a general rule, it is impossible to follow it up, for the typical bush of South Africa is the mimosa, which is smothered with sharp-pointed thorns sticking out at all angles, and anything from an inch to eight inches in length. These bushes are usually low, and throw out a pro-fusion of branches, and so closely together do they often grow that they become intertwined, making it impossible for a man to penetrate through them.

The sinuous bodies of the wild cats are, however, specially adapted for gliding under and through the densest of South African bush and undergrowth. In these thorny fastnesses the Caracal is safe from both man and dog, and nothing short of actually setting fire to the forest will dislodge it.

People living in the open drier parts of South Africa have but the faintest idea of the extreme difficulties with which the stock farmer has to contend who lives in the neighbourhood of these dense thorny forests, which furnish such ideal cover for destructive carnivorous animals.

A large male Rooi-kat is more to be feared than a leopard. The latter if disturbed at his meal will make off instantly, as a general rule. On the contrary, should the Rooi-kat be surprised in his native haunts in the act of devouring his prey, he will as likely as not spring upon the disturber of his meal. I have known of several cases of Europeans and natives being frightfully mauled by these cats. A farmer in the western part of the Cape Province was wending his way homeward by a forest path, when he surprised a Caracal busy devouring a small antelope. Without even a warning growl it leaped upon his chest and endeavoured to grip him by the throat. He, however, managed to hold it off from that vital part. After a terrible struggle he managed to get out his clasp-knife, and had to actually sever the animal's head from its body before he could release its jaws, which had a firm grip on his chest, the large canine teeth being buried deep in his chest muscles. Even after the head was completely severed from the body the grip remained as firm as ever. The only way by which he could disengage the jaws was by actually carving away the muscles of the jaws, which were set and rigid. The farmer reached home in a terrible condition. His face was seamed with deep scratches, his chest was badly bitten and torn, and the fronts of his thighs dreadfully lacerated by the claws of the animal's hind feet.

Another farmer was attacked in a similar manner by a half-grown Caracal. He was walking past some bushes at dusk, and saw something move.

Pushing the branches aside with his right arm to obtain a clearer view, the cat, without any warning, sprang at him. He raised his arm to save his face, but the ferocious animal drove its claws into his arm and shoulder and buried its teeth deeply into the muscles of the forearm, and held on as grimly as a bulldog. The man actually staggered to the homestead, a distance of over two hundred yards, with the cat fastened on to his arm, and its claws tearing viciously at his side. In this instance, too, the head had to be severed from the body of the animal, and the jaws forced open with a sharp-pointed piece of iron. Unfortunately blood-poisoning set in a week or two after the occurrence, and the farmer died.

The Rooi-kat sometimes attacks and kills full-grown ostriches, both at night and in broad day-light, usually when the birds are sitting on their eggs. A farmer of my acquaintance lost an ostrich cock which he had purchased for £80. It was taking its turn on a nest of eggs in a paddock one night, when a Caracal sprang upon it and crushed its neckbones to pulp, and dined off a portion of the body. The carcase was subsequently injected with a solution of strychnine, and the cat, returning to feed again the following night, was poisoned, and its body was found at a distance of a hundred yards from the remains of the dead ostrich.

On another occasion when staying at a farm I heard a shout from one of the farm labourers, and

The Mimosa, the typical bush of South Africa.

The Mimosa, which frequently grows in dense thickets, affording sanctuary to the Rooi-kat or Caracal and others of the cat tribe whose sinuous bodies can glide with impunity under the terrible array of thorns.

A Caracal or Rooi-kat emerging from a thicket-covered cavern.

saw a large Rooi-kat bound off towards an adjacent thorny thicket. Although it was early in the afternoon, it had ventured forth a considerable distance across the veld and attacked and killed an ostrich hen while sitting on her eggs. It shattered the vertebræ of her neck with a single bite. We subsequently organised a hunt with a number of Kafirs and other folk of every shade of colour, and with as many dogs as they could muster among them, these coloured gentry spread out in crescent form and entered a large patch of bush on a rocky hillside, shouting, yelling, and pitching stones into every clump of extra thick scrub. In this manner they slowly advanced in the direction of the men with the guns, who had hidden themselves away in front so as to command the open spaces. Eventually a female Rooi-kat was shot while attempting to gain sanctuary in a wooded kloof, and a large and powerful male was chased by the dogs, and after killing and maiming a few, it sought refuge up a tree, and was then easily shot. When brought to bay in the open the Caracal, especially the male, fights furiously with its talons and teeth, making a peculiar spitting noise, very similar to that of a domestic cat, but the sound is ever so much louder.

Sometimes these cats make their lair in the hollow interior of an old forest tree. In these cavities the young are often born and reared.

At other times the kittens are reared on the ground

159

in a bed of decaying leaves in the centre of a dense, thorny thicket, or amongst the roots of a large forest tree; and at other times in fissures amongst rocks, in caverns, or in holes under boulders in the sides of scrub-covered kloofs. Occasionally the rightful occupant of an Aard Vark hole is eaten, and the hole utilised by these cats for the rearing of a family.

The number of kittens at a birth averages two to three, but occasionally as many as five are born. The mother is bold and fierce in defence of her young, and if attacked by dogs, refuses to desert her kittens, and sacrifices her life in their defence. At these times she will even attack a man.

The Rooi-kat is exceedingly agile, and rivals the Serval in this respect. Stalking a game bird it makes a rapid rush, and as the terrified bird rises on the wing it leaps into the air after it to a height of six or eight feet, and frequently succeeds in striking and securing it with its forepaws, which are armed with sharp curved claws. Dashing suddenly amongst a flock of birds, it usually succeeds in knocking several down.

A common but cruel amusement practised in the past in India was to suddenly release a pair of tame Caracals in a courtyard where a flock of pigeons had gathered to feed upon corn scattered on the ground. The cats would instantly dash among the birds, and often struck down a score or more between them. Bets were laid by the onlookers as to the number of pigeons which the animals would succeed in killing.

The Caracal when taken into captivity during the kittenhood stage of life is easily tamed, and becomes exceedingly docile and affectionate. A friend had a half-grown one which ran about the house like any domestic cat, and knew its name so well that it always responded when called. Many years ago, before my arrival at the Port Elizabeth Museum, a tame Rooi-kat roamed through the building at all times and made friends with any visitor who happened to make kindly overtures. It never did any damage, and was not known to have interfered with anyone. Occasionally it ventured out into the street, but bolted back into the museum in wild alarm on the approach of a strange dog.

When captured very young they are difficult to rear, often refusing to take milk, and when forcibly fed they do not thrive. An animal dealer of my acquaintance was very unsuccessful in rearing young Caracals, which he always kept confined in cages, until I suggested constructing a large enclosure for them, in which to take exercise in the sunshine and fresh air. He did so, and had no further difficulty.

The Bechuana natives make excellent skin rugs, known as karosses, from the pelts of these Rooi-kats. Sometimes an entire kaross is made from the skins, and at other times one only is set in the centre, and bordered with the skins of other animals. The Bechuanas believe that if a Rooi-kat kaross is worn it will cure rheumatism. The fat of the animal is also greatly sought after by them as an ointment for the treatment of the same disease.

In Northern Africa the Caracal attains a greater average size than those in South Africa, and is in consequence recognised as a sub-species (*Felis caracal berberorum*).

An adult male Caracal is as large as a Collie dog or a rather small-sized leopard. It is long in the legs, of comparatively slender build, uniform brick red in colour, fur thick, ears sharp-pointed and tipped with tufts of long black hairs. The largest specimen which I have so far seen was shot in the Addo bush near Port Elizabeth in 1912. It measured thirty-seven inches from nose to root of tail. Length of the tail was twelve inches, and height at the shoulder twenty and a half inches.

In South Africa the Caracal occurs chiefly in the Cape Province, both west and east, and the Kalahari, Bechuanaland, and German South-west Africa. In the Orange Free State, Transvaal, and Rhodesia it is less frequently met with, and in Natal it is unknown.

THE HUNTING LEOPARD

(Cynælurus jubatus)

Also known as the Chita or Cheetah, Luipard, or Vlackte
tijger; Ngulule of Zulus (*Drummond*); Shlozi of
Amaxosa (*Cloete*); Nki or Nkwani of Bechuanas
(*Smith*); Sigakaka of Basutos (*Kirby*); Ihlozi of Swazis

THE Hunting Leopard must not be confused with
the real Leopard, which in South Africa is popularly known as a Tiger. It is so very different from
the true leopard in a variety of ways that naturalists
have been obliged to create a new genus for it.

The true cats, which are all similar in tooth and
claw formation, are grouped under one genus, viz.
Felis. The genus in which the Hunting Leopard
is placed is known as *Cynælurus*, which means
" dog-cat," so called because this animal possesses
some of the characteristics of the dog tribe, and
can be aptly described as a creature which is one
part dog and three parts cat.

All the true cats have sharp curved talons or
claws that are retractile, which means they can
be withdrawn into sockets in the toes so as to be
invisible.

163

NATURAL HISTORY OF SOUTH AFRICA

On the contrary, the claws of the Hunting Leopard can only be slightly withdrawn, and are at all times visible, like those of a dog. These claws are comparatively blunt, and not so acutely curved as those of the true cats. In addition it resembles the dog in certain of its teeth and muscles.

At a first glance a Chita has the appearance of a lanky, half-starved leopard. On close inspection, however, it is seen to be a slender, graceful animal, the body and long limbs being specially built for speed. Even the chest is modified in a special way to aid in giving the animal the maximum degree of speed, for it is very narrow and eminently adapted to cleave the air with the smallest amount of resistance.

Apart from its long legs and slender body, the Hunting Leopard differs from the true leopard in its exterior appearance, it being covered all over with black spots, instead of spots arranged in rosette shape, as on the leopard. The general colour of the animal is more or less similar to that of the leopard, being tawny or ochre yellow.

There is only one species of Chita or Hunting Leopard, although a slight difference exists between those of South Africa and those inhabiting India. The former are somewhat more robust than the latter.

The Chita inhabits the whole of Africa from the Cape to the Mediterranean Ocean, and extends eastwards to India, where it is common.

THE HUNTING LEOPARD

In South Africa this animal, in the past, was partial to the grass-covered plains, especially those parts covered with scattered bush, and avoided dense forests and damp localities. This would naturally be so, for its mode of capturing its prey is to creep up as near to it as possible, and make a sudden rush, for the Chita is the fleetest of all animals for short distances of about five hundred yards. If it should succeed in stealing up within a hundred yards or so of an antelope out on the grassy veld, there would be little or no hope of escape for the creature, for the Chita, travelling at twice the speed of the buck, would soon come abreast of it, and, seizing it by the throat, would at once drag it to the ground. Should it fail in its first rush, it gives up the chase, knowing full well that continued pursuit would be hopeless.

In many parts of South Africa, where in the past Hunting Leopards were common, they have entirely vanished, and in other parts are more or less rare, having so far avoided extermination by taking refuge in the forests and secluded wooded kloofs. In favourable localities in the upper parts of South Africa where there is ample cover, particularly in the Kalahari and other places where the hunter seldom ventures, the Hunting Leopard is still comparatively common. In Southern Rhodesia they are so numerous that they do a considerable amount of harm by harrying the flocks and herds of the pioneer farmers. Rewards are offered by the Government of that country for their destruction, and in 1911 awards were given for fifty Hunting Leopards. The natural prey of these carnivorous animals consists of various species of antelopes, small animals, such for instance as hares, and the larger game birds. If a stock farmer should elect to settle down within the hunting-grounds of a Chita, he must make up his mind to hunt down, kill, or poison the beast, or else submit to his stock being constantly raided by this famous hunter of the plains.

The name Vlackte tijger given to this animal by the Dutch voortrekkers is very appropriate, for it means " the tiger of the plains." Except when frequently hunted or when in the neighbourhood of man, the Chita hunts by day, and seems most active during cloudy weather. In the wild parts of South Africa seldom traversed by civilised man, the Chita still frequents the open grassy veld, or where the ground is sparsely covered with low scrubby bush. However, it is an exceedingly shy and secretive animal, and carefully avoids its most dreaded of enemies—man, for when he makes his appearance and settles down upon the land, it retires into the more broken bushy parts of the country. From these secure retreats it ranges forth at nights in search of prey, and harries the flocks and herds of the settler.

In a dark, rugged, bush-covered kloof in the Drakensberg Mountains in Natal, we once located a pair of Chitas. They inhabited a large cavity

The Hunting Leopard or Chita, which is the swiftest of all the cat tribe. It is longer in the legs than an ordinary leopard, and more slender in body. Note the claws which, unlike those of the true leopard, are not retractile.

under a mass of overhanging rocks. In the darkness at the extreme end of the lair we could see their eyes, which flashed a lurid green. The dogs barked furiously, and the great cats answered with a series of snarls and deep grunts. Climbing round a ledge of rock, an old Zulu servant, who was armed with a percussion cap muzzle-loading gun charged with a double dose of powder and half a handful of leaden slugs, blazed point-blank at one of the Chitas, shattering its skull and killing it instantly. Its mate at once bounded out and vanished into the bushes before we recovered our presence of mind. We followed its trail with the aid of our dogs, and eventually located it up a forest tree, lying flat along a large branch on to which it had evidently sprung with a single leap from the ground.

Unless wounded and cornered a Hunting Leopard will not attempt to attack a man, so great is its dread of him. Major F. G. Alexander, who has hunted these animals in India, and has considerable experience of them, says: " I have good reason to know that in their wild state they are, when wounded, most dangerous animals, and even when mortally wounded will do their best to reach you : in fact I would rather face a charging tiger or leopard on foot than a Chita."

In India at the present day and from prehistoric times Chitas are, and have been, tamed, and most of the Indian princes and many of the nobility own one or more.

They are so tame that their attendants, the Pathans, take them out regularly on leash for exercise, without any muzzle or hood, in the same way as we take large dogs out for a walk. The people take no more heed of them than they would if they were ordinary domestic dogs, and show not the slightest fear of them.

These Chitas are very easily tamed, and become docile and gentle, although they are rather excitable in disposition.

When required for hunting purposes, as is usually the case in India, the Chita is caught when adult, or nearly so, as it is stated the kittens can never be taught to hunt unless they learn the art from their mother. It takes about six months to tame and train a Chita to hunt in the manner required of it by its master. The male is always preferred for hunting purposes.

The Chitas when required for a hunt are led out on leash, and a hood, similar to the kind used for falcons, is placed on the head. The animals are then put on to an uncovered bullock cart, with two attendants in charge of each animal—one on each side of it. When being thus conveyed the animals usually sit on their haunches like great dogs.

The Chitas at this time are very hungry, for, previous to a hunt, they are deprived of food for about twenty-four hours. When several Chitas are used, the carts containing them are kept parallel at a distance of about two hundred yards from each other when the game preserves are reached. The attendants keep a sharp look-out, and when one of them sights a buck he moves forward, and the other carts are at once pulled up and remain at a standstill. When the cart gets within about a hundred and fifty yards of the buck, the Chita's hood is raised, and its attention directed to the quarry. The leash is then removed, and the animal, springing lightly to the ground, crouches low and carefully and noiselessly stalks the buck, moving at a slow pace in characteristic cat fashion, until the animal becomes alarmed and gallops off. The cat, whose eyes were never for one instant off its intended victim, seeing it making off, springs forward and races after the quarry, covering the ground in a succession of long, rapid, low bounds, at the speed of something like a mile a minute. Overtaking the buck it grips it by the throat and holds fast bulldog fashion, until the arrival of the Pathan keepers, one of whom opens a large vein in the inner side of the back leg of the victim and fills a wooden ladle with the blood. This ladle of blood is then handed to the other, or chief keeper, who offers it to the Chita, whose grip on the throat of the buck has not relaxed in the slightest. The sight and smell of the blood causes the Chita to instantly release its hold, and while it is greedily lapping up the warm blood, the second keeper drags the body of the victim away to a distance, while his colleague slips the hood over the Chita's head when its attention is occupied in lapping up the blood. The leash is then secured to its collar, and it once again takes its place on the cart, and is usually not used again that day.

Should the buck outdistance its pursuer in the first five hundred yards or so, the animal gives up the chase and awaits the arrival of its keepers and the cart.

After the day's hunt is over the hungry Chitas are fed liberally with the flesh of their victims.

The word " tiger " in South Africa is applied to both the true Leopard and Hunting Leopard. In India the word Chita is also applied to both of these animals, and consequently causes much confusion; therefore it is best that this animal should be known as the Hunting Leopard.

A Hunting Leopard resting. These animals are trained in India to hunt antelopes.

CLASSIFICATION OF THE ANIMALS MENTIONED IN THIS BOOK

Class : MAMMALIA

Order : PRIMATES
(Man, Apes, and Lemurs)

Sub-order : ANTHROPOIDEA
(Includes Man, Anthropoid (Man-like) Apes, and Monkeys)

Family : CERCOPITHECIDÆ
(Old-World Monkeys and Baboons)

The whole of the Monkeys of the Old World, with the exception of the Anthropoid or man-like Apes, are included in this family. They are distinguished from most of the New-World (American) Monkeys by having bare callosities on the buttocks and by the presence of cheek pouches or sacculated stomachs. In a considerable number of the American Monkeys the tail is prehensile. It is not so in any of the Old-World Monkeys.

Species

(Inhabiting South Africa)

1. *Cercopithecus labiatus,* Is. Geoff. *C.R. Acad. Sci.,* **xv.** p. 1038 (1842).
2. *Cercopithecus stairsi mossambicus,* Pocock. *P.Z.S.,* 1907, p. 705.
3. *Cercopithecus albogularis,* Sykes.
3a. *Cercopithecus albogularis beirensis,* Pocock. *P.Z.S,,* 1907, p. 701.
4. *Cercopithecus pygerythrus,* Cuv.

NATURAL HISTORY OF SOUTH AFRICA

4a. Cercopithecus pygerythrus rufoviridis, .Is. Geoff. *C.R. Acad Sci.*, xv. p. 1038 (1842).

5. *Papio porcarius*, Bodd.
5a. Papio porcarius griseipes, Pocock. *P.Z.S.*, 1911, p. 558.
6. *Papio cynocephalus*, Is. Geoff.

Sub-order : LEMUROIDÆ ·

Family : LEMURIDÆ

Sub-family : *Galaginæ*

(*The Galagos*)

The members of this sub-family have exceptionally large ears, which are nearly destitute of fur, and capable of being folded down as desired by the animal. Tail long and bushy ; eyes large. The chief skeletal condition which separates them from others of the Lemur group is the lengthening of the calcaneum and naviculare in the ankle.

In the sub-family *Galaginæ* there are three genera in Madagascar, viz. *Apolemur, Microcebus,* and *Chirogale* ; and in Africa one genus, viz. *Galago.*

The headquarters of the Lemur tribe is the island of Madagascar, where they represent one-half of the entire fauna.

A few species are found in Africa, Southern India, Ceylon, and as far east as the Celebes and Philippines.

Species

(Inhabiting South Africa)

1. *Galago crassicaudatus*, Is. Geoff. *Ann. Mus.*, xix. p. 166 (1812).
2. *Galago garnetti*, Ogilby.
3. *Galago moholi*, Smith.
4. *Galago granti*, Thos. and Wrought. *P.Z.S.*, 1907, p. 286.
5. *Galago mossambicus*, Pet.
6. *Galago zuluensis*, Elliott. *Ann. Mag. Nat. Hist.* (7), xx. p. 186 (1907).

172

CLASSIFICATION OF ANIMALS

Order : **CHIROPTERA**

(The Bat Tribe)

Sub-order : MEGACHIROPTERA

(The Frugivorous or Fruit-eating Bats)

Family : PTEROPODIDÆ

This family contains all the Frugivorous or Fruit-eating Bats. They are usually of large size; the molar teeth are not tubercular, the crowns being smooth, but marked with a deep longitudinal furrow; the palate is continued behind the last molars; the second finger usually terminates in a claw (always, in the South African species of Fruit Bats). The two edges of the ear are in contact at the base, so as to form a complete ring. Tail, when present, has no connection with the wing membrane. The members of this family are restricted to the warmer parts of the Old World.

Species

(Inhabiting South Africa)

1. *Epomophorus wahlbergi*, Sund. *Oefvers. Akad. Förhandl.,* *Stockholm,* 1846, p. 118 (1847).
2. *Epomophorus crypturus*, Pet.
3. *Epomophorus angolensis*, Gray. *Catal*, 1870, p. 125.
4. *Eidolon helvum*, Kerr. *Animal Kingdom,* i. pl. i., p. xvii. 91, No. 108.
5. *Rousettus leachi*, A. Smith. *Zool. Journ.,* iv. p. 443.

Sub-order : MICROCHIROPTERA

(The Insectivorous or Insect-eating Bat Tribe)

Family : RHINOLOPHIDÆ

(*The Horse-shoe and Leaf-nosed Bats*)

Small Insectivorous Bats with leafy outgrowths around the nostrils; ears large, without a tragus; under finger minus a phalanx. These Bats range over Africa, Asia, and Australia. They are not represented in Europe.

Species
(Inhabiting South Africa)

1. *Rhinolophus simulator*, K. And. *Ann. Mag. Nat. Hist.* (7), xiv. p. 384 (1904).
2. *Rhinolophus denti*, Thos. *Ann. Mag. Nat. Hist.* (7), xiii. p. 386 (1904).
3. *Rhinolophus capensis*, Licht.
4. *Rhinolophus darlingi*, K. And. *Ann. Mag. Nat. Hist.* (7), xv. p. 21 (1905).
5. *Rhinolophus augur typicus*, K. And. *Ann. Mag. Nat. Hist.* (7), xiv. p. 380 (1904).
5a. *Rhinolophus augur zuluensis*, K. And. *Ann. Mag. Nat. Hist.* (7), xiv. p. 383 (1904).
5b. *Rhinolophus augur zambesiensis*, K. And. *Ann. Mag. Nat. Hist.* (7), xiv. p. 383 (1904).
6. *Rhinolophus empusa*, K. And. *Ann. Mag. Nat. Hist.* (7), xiv. p. 378 (1904) ; Chubb, *P.Z.S.*, 1909, p. 115.
7 *Rhinolophus lobatus*, Pet. *Reise Mosambique Säugeth.*, p. 41, pls. ix., xiii., figs. 16, 17 (1852).
8. *Rhinolophus æthiops*, Pet.
9. *Rhinolophus hildebrandti*, Pet.
10. *Rhinolophus swinnyi*, Gough. *Ann. Trans. Mus.*, i. No. I., p. 71 (1908).
11. *Clæotis percivali*, Thos. *Ann. Mag. Nat. Hist.* (7), viii. p. 28 (1901) ; Chubb, *P.Z.S.*, 1909, p. 115.
12. *Hipposiderus caffer*, Sund.
13. *Hipposiderus commersoni*, Schreb.

Family : NYCTERIDÆ
(The False Vampire and Slit-faced Bats)

The Bats of this family are distinguished from those of the preceding family by the presence of a small but well-developed tragus in the ears, which are long, and in the nose-leaf not being so complicated. In those forming the typical genus it is practically absent, and is represented by a slit running down the middle of the face; hence the name Slit-faced Bats. The only Bats representing this family in South Africa belong to this genus (*Nycteris*). The members of this family are confined to Africa, Asia, and the Malay States.

CLASSIFICATION OF ANIMALS

Species
(Inhabiting South Africa)

1. *Nycteris capensis*, A. Smith.
2. *Nycteris hispida*, Geoff.
3. *Nycteris thebaica*, Geoff.

Family : VESPERTILIONIDÆ
(The Serotine Bats)

In this family of Insectivorous Bats the nostrils are at the extremity of the snout and form simple crescentic or circular apertures ; there is no nose-leaf ; ears moderate, with distinct inner tragus. The tail is comparatively long, and is included in the membrane which joins the short hind legs.

The Bats which form this very extensive family are practically cosmopolitan in their distribution.

Species
(Inhabiting South Africa)

1. *Eptesicus capensis*, A. Smith.
1a. *Eptesicus capensis gracilior*, Thos. and Schw. *P.Z.S.,* 1905, i. p. 257.
1b. *Eptesicus megalurus*, Temm.
2. *Pipistrellus nanus*, Pet.
2a. *Pipistrellus nanus australis. Ann. Trans. Mus.,* iv. (1913).
3. *Pipistrellus kuhlii fuscatus*, Thos. *Ann. Mag. Nat. Hist.* (7), viii. p. 34 (1901).
4. *Pipistrellus subtilis*, Sund. *Ofv. Akad. Förh.,* 1846, p. 119.
5. *Pipistrellus rusticus*, Tomes. *Ann. Mag. Nat. Hist.* (8), vol. iv.
6. *Glauconycteris variegatus*, Tomes.
7. *Glauconycteris papilo*, Thos. *Ann. Mag. Nat. Hist.* (7), xv. p. 77 (1905).
8. *Scotophilus nigrita*, Schreb.,
8a. *Scotophilus nigrita dingani*, Pet. *South African Journ.,* 1832, p. 27.

175

NATURAL HISTORY OF SOUTH AFRICA

8b. *Scotophilus nigrita herero*, Thos. *Ann. Mag. Nat. Hist.* (7), xvii. p. 174 (1906).

9. *Scotophilus viridis damarensis*, Thos. *Ann. Mag. Nat. Hist.* (7), xvii. p. 174 (1906).

10. *Scotophilus schlieffeni australis*, Thos. and Wrought. *P Z.S.*, 1908, p. 539.

11. *Myotis tricolor*, Smuts.

12. *Kerivoula ærosa*, Tomes.

13. *Kerivoula lanosa*, Smith.

14. *Miniopterus schreibersi*, Natt.

15. *Miniopterus dasythrix*, Temm. *Mon. Mamm.*, ii. p. 174 (1835).

16. *Miniopterus natalensis*, Smith. *S.A. Quart. Journ.*, ii. p. 59 (1834).

17. *Miniopterus scoteinus*, Sund.

18. *Miniopterus fraterculus*, Thos. and Schw. *P.Z.S.*, 1906, i. p. 162.

19. *Taphozous mauritianus*, Geoff.

20. *Nyctinomus africanus*, Dobs.

21. *Nyctinomus ægyptiacus*, Geoff.

22. *Nyctinomus bocagei*, Seabra. *Jorn. Sc. Lisb.*, vi. p. 82 (1900).

23. *Mormopterus acetabulosus*, Desm.

24. *Chærephon limbatus*, Pet.

Order : **CARNIVORA**
(The Flesh-eating Tribe of Animals)
Sub-order : FISSIPEDIA
Division : ÆLUROIDEA
Family : FELIDÆ
(*The Cat Tribe*)

Carnivorous animals that walk on the tips of the toes (digitigrade) ; fore limbs provided with five, and the hind limbs with four toes ; claws are usually curved, sharp, and retractile, viz. capable of being drawn back into special sheaths in the toes. Skull short, broad, and rounded, with the auditory bullæ large, smooth, and inflated. Canine teeth

176

strongly developed ; one pair of molars in upper and lower jaws ; three small incisors above and below.

This family is cosmopolitan, with the exception of Madagascar and the Australian region.

Species
(Inhabiting South Africa)

1. *Felis leo*, Linn.
2. *Felis pardus*, Linn.
3. *Felis serval*, Erxl.
4. *Felis nigripes*, Burch.
5. *Felis ocreata cafra*, Desm.
6 *Felis caracal*, Guld.
7. *Cynælurus jubatus*, Erxl.

ALPHABETICAL INDEX

PRINTED IN GREAT BRITAIN BY NEILL AND CO, LTD, EDINBURGH.

Milton Keynes UK
Ingram Content Group UK Ltd.
UKHW022248080124
435706UK00005B/344